# DOES THE MIND SHAPE REALITY?

## THE PROCESS OF TRUTH DISCOVERY ENABLES FREEDOM THROUGH COMPLETE CONTROL OF HUMAN PERCEPTION

SUPRITAM BASU
DIPTI BASU MONDAL

Those who have mustered the courage to explore this possibility will find
this text. The thoughts, imaginations, meanderings, and restlessness of
souls who defy reality as they see it are addressed in this book. Seekers
who use their skepticism to challenge everything they know about the
world are what this book intends for. This book is for you. These words
bring forth the audacity to welcome uncertain futures.

# Contents


*Foreword* — *vii*

*Preface* — *ix*

*Acknowledgements* — *xi*

*Prologue* — *xiii*

1. Breaking The Illusion: The Invisible Script Of Life — 1

2. Transcending The Mind: The Path To True Awareness — 16

3. Unlearning To Be: "Breaking Free From The Illusion Of Control" — 25

4. The Space Between Thoughts — 35

5. The Mastery Of Destiny: A Conversation On Fate And Free Will — 40

6. Psychology Of Self-understanding — 46

7. The Art Of Concentration — 52

8. Establish Only Three Main Goals Per Day — 64

9. Failure Patterns Persist With Solutions — 78

10. The Hidden Truth Behind Forgetting — 87

11. The Hidden Whispers Of Forgetfulness — 90

12. The Echoes Of Not Remembering — 93

13. The Power Of Forgetting — 96

14. Missteps In Reading And Writing — 107

15. The Strange Nature Of Forgetting — 111

16. Mistakes In Action – When We Get In Our Own Way — 119

17. The Hidden Meanings Behind Our Actions — 126

18. Challenging To Clarify Experiences — 147

19. The Power Of Silence — 152

20. Finding Tranquility In A Noisy World — 153

21. The Practice Of Silence Enables You To Develop Inner Peace During — 154

22. Silence As A Tool For Self-Reflection — 156

23. The Healing Power Of Silence — 157

24. Maximizing Productivity Through Silence — 161

# Contents


25. INTRODUCTION TO MINDFULNESS     165

26. The Hidden Storehouse Of Memories     170

27. Making Conscious Choices     174

Final Thoughts     183

# FOREWORD

Literature includes educational material that teaches knowledge yet also exists with books guiding unlearning processes. The mind functions as a powerful system which builds our awareness of the world but people usually fail to examine if its core elements are genuine. Through mental patterns along with perceptual habits and elusive premises humans determine their life possibilities. Every assumption humans hold about reality seems to exist as an output of the mental functions. "Does the Mind Shape Reality?" is not a book of conclusions. This book takes readers on an unrestricted path to discover the inner facts about how we perceive things and maintain consciousness as we navigate the essence of existence. The text rejects the common view that wisdom should be obtained through education because it proposes wisdom needs to be completely transcended. Reading this work involves more than word assimilation because you will face deep questions which emerge from the word gaps. Anyone who experienced heavy burdens from existence alongside mind-related questions should find a valuable discussion within the pages of this book. Come read the content without any expectations because your view will remain open. Profound epiphanies show themselves through freedom from the need for answers rather than solutions.

# Preface

A narrative surrounds our existence starting before our birth and lasting beyond our time. Our childhood introduction to names along with beliefs structures and identities develops into a single script that identifies our identity. Our life unfolds as we believe the existing story to be genuine. Our lives follow its regulations and we hunt after its benefits and we constantly worry about its negative results. But at some point, some of us stop. We pause. Reflection reveals that the world possibly lacks everything we currently perceive. A simple mental whisper turned into asking questions which became the spark that started the journey recounted in this book. The purpose of this text is not to teach but to eliminate what proves useless. Within these words, an alternative exists from both guidance and philosophy. The text promotes a new way of thinking by allowing free unlearning while accepting that everything flows without fixed boundaries. Spend ample time reading through every word. Let them sink in. Exercise the most essential step by releasing these words. You should release truth since it exists independently from your grasp. It is something to experience.

# ACKNOWLEDGEMENTS

No thought exists in isolation. Every statement we utter along with each intellectual discovery emerges from numerous hidden connections that stem from spoken dialogues complex challenges social meetings and internal contemplation. This book is no exception. You thinkers along with writers whose intellectual contributions transformed me will continue to guide my path as a lantern shines in darkness. My friends together with my loved ones provided the environment to doubt my beliefs alongside patience to hear my uncertainties while delivering the needed honesty for healthy questioning. My work became deep through all of the debates we shared all the late-night conversations that we held and all the moments of mutual curiosity. To the reader—thank you for your presence here. The messages contained in these pages travel only halfway in their own right since your open-minded exploration makes up the remaining path toward meaningful self-expression. The true meaning emerges solely from the emptiness that develops between statements and the absence of words. Everything would remain nonexistent if not for silence.

# PROLOGUE

Every person experiences a time during their life when previously known things suddenly show unfamiliarity. Each day starts with you observing your surroundings before understanding the world seems different from its previous state. The structures alongside beliefs and rules seem artificial since they were placed upon you instead of emerging from your own choice. Such an awareness marks the commencement of mental development. Getting enlightenment through awakening requires more than comfortable circumstances. It is unsettling. The process of waking from belief involves allowing formerly certain things to reveal their illusory nature. One understands reality exists only through the shaping influence of the mind which observes and interprets it. The presented book does not present itself as a vessel of factual knowledge. The text guides you toward breaking free from truth altogether. Welcome to those who.seek freedom from mental bounds while investigating their mental processes. This book exists to recall information you have always held rather than delivering information for new knowledge. Step forward. The book guides its readers to experience the world after abandoning their quest for answers.

# I

# Breaking the Illusion: The Invisible Script of Life

The Illusion of Moreh your mind. They will linger. They will shift and move within you, the way wind moves through open space.

And maybe, just maybe, that's where life truly begins.

Do you ever feel like we are bound to a life that is just one big list of rules? Do we all feel that way? From the moment we are born, it's as if we are handed an invisible guidebook—what to do right, what not to do, what's wrong. And it's everywhere—religion, society, even in the way we talk to each other.

I get it. We need some kind of structure. But at what point does guidance turn into a cage?

Think about it. Every sacred book talks about compassion and love, truth, and the purpose of life. But here's the thing: does wisdom tell us how to live, or does it walk with us as we figure it out?

Compassion—real love—isn't about controlling or fixing people. It's not about giving them a set of instructions. It doesn't sugarcoat reality just to make it easier to swallow. It's not about making someone comfortable; it's about being real with them.

So why do we hold back? Why do we filter our words, soften our thoughts, or stay silent just because we're scared of saying the wrong things? Imagine two people just... existing together. Do you ever see an animal hesitate before showing emotion?

No lemon plant wants to become a mango tree. They know themselves—they just want to have a fulfilling life.

Just being yourself—talking, observing—no fear, no walls, no pressure to be right or perfect. Just honesty.

It sounds almost impossible, right? But maybe that's because we've made it that way. Maybe we've been taught that truth should be packaged neatly, that love should always be soft, that life should always make sense. But it doesn't.

Maybe wisdom isn't something to follow. Maybe it's something to experience—to sit with, to question, to grow into. Maybe we don't need more answers. Maybe we just need more space to be.

Why does the mind feel like an endless illusion? Why do we keep searching for ways to control it, shape it, and turn it into a tool for success? Everyone wants answers, but are they truly looking for truth, or just something that fits neatly into what they already believe?

From the moment we step into the world, we are handed a script—taught how to think, how to live, and what to strive for. Life becomes a set of choices, but only from a pre-approved list. Step outside of it, and suddenly, you're lost. But is that really being lost, or is it the first step toward freedom?

Somewhere along the way, life has started to feel hollow—like a machine running on autopilot. People move through their days, playing roles they never questioned, following patterns set long before them. Love, curiosity, and openness slowly get buried under ambition, expectation, and fear. Instead of exploring life, we defend our cages, mistaking them for security.

To be in a world like this is difficult. It means questioning things others take for granted. It means being seen as uncertain, doubtful—maybe even weak. But what's the alternative? To live within a rigid, self-contained box? To mistake repetition for meaning?

That kind of existence may feel safe, but it is limited—closed off from the vastness of what life could be.

So, what will you choose? Will you continue walking the same well-designed roads, picking from the same set of options, or will you step into the unknown? Not for the sake of rebellion, but simply to see for yourself—to live in a way that isn't dictated by invisible walls.

Because if you're truly ready, these words won't just pass through.

Sometimes, there's a longing to be lost. To step away from the clear, structured roads that feel too predictable. But the mind resists—it questions, it pushes against the edge, always testing the boundaries. How far can I go?

How much can I understand? It turns inward, measuring its own limits of thought, of feeling, of imagination—only to solve the problems it created and celebrate its own cleverness.

But what if we stop trying to solve and simply step into the unknown?

We talk about simplicity as if it's freedom, but sometimes, simplicity becomes a cage. A bird sits inside, not because it was trapped, but because it built the bars itself. And now, it fears the sky.

If we cannot, then what will we do?

The mind whispers endlessly. It plays out every possibility, every scenario, until it is exhausted—watching life through the small window of its own making, waiting to be freed.

But freed by whom?

There is no captor. No external force keeping it in place. It is a bird in a self-made prison, sitting in the vastness of nothingness. The cage, the emptiness, even the struggle—it all exists within the mind.

And yet, it still asks: Is there more?

Not out of surrender, not out of a deep desire to dissolve into the vastness, but from a place of acquisition. Not to lose itself, but to collect more—more achievements, more knowledge, more titles, more rare jewels to decorate the ever-growing illusion of self.

But maybe real freedom isn't about adding anything at all. Maybe it's about daring to open the cage door—and finally fly.

What Does 'More' Truly Mean?

Have you ever thought about what the term more truly signifies?

Money and fame, along with increasing social media popularity, are nothing more than different forms of the same craving—just different flavors.

But really? That's something else.

New knowledge doesn't come from upgrading what we already know. It arrives from uncharted territories. It's not about adding—it's about seeing.

We chase. We want to. We reach. And yet, purpose remains an unanswered question. If desire could ever truly satisfy us, wouldn't it have done so by now?

Words themselves don't provide direction. They function like hands pointing at the moon, not the moon itself.

But love—that's different. Love is a state of purity, without competition or the constant push and pull. Just being.

And in understanding this, we realize: the separate pieces never actually existed.

It was all one. Always.

The whole universe contains only one essential more—the only one that truly matters.

Is Thinking the Problem?

People try to shape their thinking into boxes, as if controlling it makes it real.

Every human being questions themselves: What am I?

But is that the real issue?

Maybe what truly matters is not what we are, but the fact that we even ask at all.

What if we stopped resisting? What if we let go of the need to analyze and simply allowed thought to flow?

That's the thing, isn't it?

My mind equals myself because I am the same as my thoughts. The moment I notice this, I start moving—upward, downward, it doesn't matter. Thinking happens. I can't force it to stop. And when it does stop, I find that I can't make it move again.

The foundation never changes.

Thinking or not thinking—it doesn't really matter. What lies deeper is not control, but the act of happening.

Living isn't about effort. It just is.

A beam of light doesn't attempt rectilinear motion.

It just moves.

And This? This Is Just a Story.

Time keeps counting.

People prove their existence through their shared presence and the events that unfold between them.

But before time? Can we even ask that?

We can't step outside of time to view it objectively.

Maybe escaping the story isn't the purpose of life. Maybe it's to know it fully.

Stopping our constant predictions and surrendering to the moment reveals an entirely new universe to our awareness. A surprise.

The water keeps flowing, constantly touching things for the first time.

The Loop

That's the loop, isn't it?

The mind follows its circular path. The original question creates a reaction, which inevitably brings us back to the same question.

And if the questions stop?

The movement discontinues. Not because presence isn't there, but because it was never really there to begin with.

We observe the mind running in circles, always reaching for an objective that it cannot grasp.

What is the proper way to approach this?

The cycle of thought begins and ends at the same point.

Beauty?

It's not in explanations.

Nothing truly beautiful can be contained by words, descriptions, or images.

It's an experience.

Wild, uncontrollable experience.

It belongs to no one. It doesn't cater to preferences.

Rain is beautiful. The sun is beautiful.

What moment isn't?

Change and existence happen together, always.

A Butterfly's Wings

A butterfly moves its wings—once.

And everything changes.

It stays still, and yet the world shifts around it.

Action isn't in movement.

It's in will.

Physical matter only disguises the truth of what lies beyond.

But then—why the emptiness?

Even after attaining everything, a question remains.

One that nothing seems to answer.

I search for guidance—a path, a teacher, a book.

But nothing helps.

The absence of an answer brings tears.

The bird takes flight, searching for the perfect tree, the perfect place to land.

But the image in its mind never matches the reality it finds.

And so, it keeps flying.

Because reality cannot be measured.

And the search?

It only ends with death.
What Is Life?
You feel it, don't you?
That movement inside you—life.
And death? That's when movement stops.
Or does it?
A drop of water falls from the mountain, becoming a river before reaching the ocean.
It changes form.
But it never stops moving.
The story continues.
So do you.
So do I.
The Flower and the Noise
A flower blooms.
It simply is.
And then, we arrived. With our words, our theories, our explanations.
Someone paints it. Someone writes about it.
Scientists dissect its petals. Philosophers search for its meaning.
And soon, the arguments begin.
Who understood it better? Whose version is correct?
But the flower?
Still just there.
Being.
Someone could sit beside it in silence.
Just watching.
Just understanding—without needing to explain.
The Game of 'I' and 'Not I'
Look around.
Everything—the world, your emotions, your thoughts—exists within you.
It happens inside your consciousness.
This is it. This is all we ever know.
'I' and 'Not I'—the dance of identity and experience.
Trying to explain beyond this?
We fail, because reality is in motion. Always pulsing, never fixed.
Some call it life. Some call it God. Some call it the soul.
Words.

Just words.

Love Is the Answer, Right?

Maybe.

To truly understand love is to realize that we are shaped by everything outside of us.

True humility isn't about saying "I am humble."

It's deeper than that.

Because in that moment—the moment we know—the separate I disappears.

All that remains is connection.

All that remains is love.

Letting go is not a one-time event; it happens constantly. Human beings acquire experiences and emotional attachments while simultaneously needing to abandon certain internal elements. What immaculate process allows us to shift between holding onto things while simultaneously granting them permission to go?

That's life too.

And God? The status of God as God arises when humanity chooses to believe in this divine power.

Money functions as money only because people have agreed to use it as such. Diamonds hold their worth because humanity created the convention that they represent value.

The meaning of everything we believe—including identity—comes from those who support our beliefs, as well as from the people who assign them value.

The authentic mystery may not be the search for truth versus falsehood.

Being here—fully—seems to be the core matter.

What do you think?

The Weight of a Story

When my story depends on someone's acceptance, the listener's power becomes equal to the storyteller's strength.

Human beings do not reside within themselves but in the interconnection that develops between them and others. Our identity stems from the love and understanding we receive from others and the acknowledgment they bestow upon us.

Every person carries burdens—the weight of personal history, identity, accomplishments, and unachieved dreams.

Time does not change this, whether we carry gold or stone; the continued burden leads only to an ongoing sense of heaviness.

Rich or poor, famous or unknown—everyone bears a heavy load.

And you feel it, don't you? We create mental boundaries that reinforce our self-made restrictions. We tell ourselves we must carry this weight because it represents our identity.

The brain diverts attention from reality. The subconscious mind uses storytelling to distract us from confronting the fundamental question that does not exist in reality:

Survival requires us to bear this weight. What's the alternative? Can I actually let go?

I should handle my weight through better management instead of attempting to shed it entirely.

My weight status makes me happy enough to accept whatever consequences may arise.

It never ends.

The genuine method of discovery? Face it. Observe the potential actions along with the unattainable ones. Try.

Human existence becomes truly sincere when we continuously question everything while understanding the difference between knowledge and belief.

That's the fuel of life.

What Goes Out, Comes In

When you distribute anger through judgment, the energy returns to you in the same form. What you hold within is what you receive—without any exchange process.

The motion of anger does not follow a direct path; it spreads, multiplying in different directions, invading both yourself and others with its fire.

Love operates the same way.

Self-love is not about mirror affirmations. One influences the universe through the volume of affection they freely share.

Love exists without motion; it simply is, without a directional tendency.

Love that dwells within you becomes available to yourself, to others, and to the world. No separation. Love and anger do not choose particular objects—they exist without division, despite common belief.

And words? Words are just sounds. They hold no significance until someone assigns meaning to them.

The value of my words depends entirely on your acceptance of them.

The ultimate realization is clear: love exists independently of any exchange. It simply is.

Love enters your being everywhere, without boundaries, once it reaches you.

Sit With Me

Not in a rush. Not as another task to complete.

We should sit as people do when they are unhurried—when they release the need to prove something.

After enduring battle, you should sit like a war-worn soldier, bearing the marks of struggle. The process of endless dedication finally leads her to peace.

Our battles remain hidden throughout the day. We fight to protect the existence of our stories, yearning for validation from others.

But right now—just sit.

Remove the resume credentials, the social profiles, and the professional standing. Strip away the armor.

The walls I lower might inspire you to lower yours, too.

The Space Between Us

Without revealing our truths beneath surface decoration, understanding each other becomes impossible.

Our reluctance to share reality prevents us from truly experiencing another's world.

We should not merely sit with people—we should exist alongside the sun, sky, birds, trees, and all existence. Not as separate pieces, but as one. There is only one state—being. No boundaries, no definitions, no restrictions.

The space where I meet you is blank, requiring no explanation.

Around the bonfire, laughter drowns out the background music.

In this space, you can be your authentic self without effort.

Silence fosters receptivity, not emptiness.

Here, the weight of "I" dissolves, relieving both you and me.

This is where we find our path.

Real communication, real connection, and real understanding emerge not just from words but from the stories they carry.

Have you ever sat alone, doing nothing, just being with your thoughts?

Existence without distractions leads to a pure state of being. Those who have experienced it know how quickly thoughts arise—one leading to another, like orchid vines spreading. Without intending to, you find yourself immersed in a forest you never meant to enter.

What if you refrained from following every thought? If you simply allowed them to flow without attachment—would they still have power?

The mind seeks to control everything, even itself.

Imagine a tree deciding to stop being a tree. Imagine trying to suppress the sun's rays. Absurd, right?

Yet we do this constantly.

We resist our own natural states. We try to eliminate anger, force happiness, and chase peace as if these things can be grasped.

Human existence becomes a perpetual war of conflicting inner forces.

As existence dissolves everything, only one question remains.

Not What is the meaning of life? Not What is the mind?

But simply:

Who is asking?

Investigate the nature of the "I" that keeps searching, doubting, and questioning. The thinker of every thought remains unidentified.

Who else can answer this for you? No words, teachers, or ideas will ever provide this fundamental answer.

It cannot be found in language.

The realization is the answer.

Running from meaning turns into a comedy. Ceasing the pursuit reveals that everything is already here.

Everything is already happening.

All water—whether river, ocean, rain, or snow—is the same substance.

It is simply water.

Same with us. Same with everything.

The outcome remains when you stop fighting your life, Just... being.

That's it. That's the silence. The silence becomes every existing sound that has existed since the beginning of time.

Life doesn't need a method. Life exists without needing any steps to reach its growth points. It just is.

When you release your resistance toward life, your conflict automatically ends because your mind stops trying to fit reality into its own ideas. At the point of inner acceptance, thoughts become one with the body. They move together, naturally.

True peace potentially exists in this definition.

Not fighting with your own self could be the definition of peace.

Have you ever paid full attention to the sound of rain? Not just heard it, but truly listened?

Raindrops do not generate any sound by themselves. Rain makes its sound by colliding with ground surfaces, as well as leaves and rooftops near you.

A kinetic partnership develops between liquid water drops and solid surfaces they meet. The collision between these two elements forms a novel, unified substance.

Everything works like this. The sunlight does not simply rise while nighttime descends effortlessly. They merge into each other so that both states maintain existence as the shift occurs.

Your existence matches precisely what you observe if you examine it closely.

Your existence exceeds both your mental processes and the physical body you occupy. You are more than a single expression of light or dark, happiness or sorrow. Every experience takes place within you, exactly where all other things emerge. Every part of the universal formation is manifested through you.

Many make the error of searching for solutions in external zones. Seeking adequate knowledge, combined with substantial wisdom and other essential elements, should lead to ultimate understanding. The process of understanding the universe mainly requires internal examination rather than an external search. It's about looking within.

**Which individual faces everything mentioned?**

Human beings seek definitions while using the term "I" to describe themselves. Personal identity exists as nothing more than accumulated elements that were never our choice. Thoughts we absorbed. Experiences we lived. Memories we carry. Human beings tightly clutch their identity while they try to mold and regulate it into something good, even though it remains out of their control.

That's where suffering begins.

We put weight on everything. Every act and every mental occurrence needs evaluation for correctness or incorrectness. Was it a success or failure? Was it meaningful or pointless? Weight has no place in the concept of karma. It's a movement. It's flowing. Letting things emerge as the experience of stopping our attempts to control each step throughout life. Dharma is a natural pattern rather than a strict code of conduct.

And yet, the mind resists. The mind wants control. Similar to a child, the mind engages in emotional displays of defiance. It doesn't listen. It doesn't sit still. We apply continuous struggle to win this fight, disciplining our thoughts and forcing order on our systems just to impose obedience. The solution may not lie in constant resistance. Perhaps the solution is letting ourselves be.

Flowing beside the river requires giving up the effort to shape its course.

Love grants access to spaces that all other things fail to reach.

**Love.**

Not love as an idea. True love conforms neither to the patterns of receiving nor giving in human relations. Love exists as the state where resistance no longer exists. Love appears when our defenses disappear, and friction is absent.

But here's the thing. We're not used to love. We're used to being told. To be shaped. To be judged.

A state of being without pressure or command can stir up irritation since we are not accustomed to this form of existence. This situation seems unnatural because it demands nothing from us.

Love exists as a necessary element from which our lives might truly benefit.

Because love isn't controlled. Love isn't force. People must not work to gain love because it exists beyond earning.

The simple definition of love is permitting things to stay in their current form.

Weightlessness, combined with the absence of resistance, allows all things to glide together in this space.

The river. The rain. The night and the day.

And you.

Hate maintains a clear position that we always understand, whereas love exists in such unpredictability that it causes most people fear. Hate presents an obvious situation, making everything clear. But love... love is vulnerable. To love means being completely exposed and taking possible steps into the unknown. And that? Most individuals are petrified by it.

People who seek complete guidance outside themselves will end up disappointed. My way can't be your way. A simple apple functions as it was designed to do without seeking to replace its identity with that of a mango. Mangoes do not make unnecessary efforts to transform into apples during their natural existence. They just... are.

Overthinking leads people into a solitary state of mind. Logic is sharp; it cuts. Defining yourself allows you to separate from others. Walls exist as mental divisions between what we want and reject, alongside physical barriers made from bricks. Who I am. Who I'm not.

What I can be. What I can't be. And those lines?

They box us in. We find ourselves completely alone despite being amid everything.

Did humans establish those limits from their own will? Or were they handed to us?

Fear makes boundaries shrink. Love?

Love stretches them wide. Releasing control creates new opportunities throughout the world. The dimensions and grandeur of a cage matter not, because it remains an enclosure nonetheless. You will experience loneliness when a cage suffocates you.

And then there's the infinite. Trying to grasp something larger than yourself results in failure because you either get overwhelmed by it or break free from it completely. The experience results in either complete self-loss or complete freedom. A fond laughing experience differs from being mocked because of this. The "I" receives isolation through one process, while another method leads to dissolution.

Throughout our lives, we focus on ownership and definition since everything belongs to someone else or to us. My thoughts, my music, my love. People often wonder about the ownership of the endless sky above Earth. Who owns the wind?

A spider creates its web through its natural process. The structure starts small to secure survival at its beginning stage. But then?

It keeps going. Ultimately, the web realizes its enclosure when it looks around to assess its situation. The creation entraps it exactly where it began.

Does this pattern we work on describe what we construct? Does creation enable us to survive, or does it simply keep us fixed in its structure? What do we truly possess after building something that restricts our movement?

Let this experience become your source of contemplation while your body allows it to move by rhythm and movement.

**A dance of sound. A dance of light. A dance of space.**

What makes it a dance? The one watching. The one listening. You. Me. Consciousness itself. The observer shares one continuous existence with the observed world. This motion continues exactly as before because all elements remain identical.

The real concern lies in determining our limits of awareness. What processes determine our ability to experience personal limitations? Maybe that's the whole journey. The search.

The curiosity. A single drop of water transforms over time into a flowing river, which becomes an ocean while also being cloud, ice, mist, and rain. And even that? Something larger contains this reality among multiple other parts. Water's exploration reveals the essence of life, which sustains everything.

Our directions come from outside sources, including individuals, systems, and regulations. And maybe that's fine. Maybe it's necessary. The way forward becomes possible only when we align with our natural direction.

Look around. No artificial noises disrupt the natural state of existence, so everything exists undisturbed. Effortless. Growing trees need no effort, just as the flowing river shows no sign of movement. A rose blooms—vulnerable and brilliant. An apple tree, small but steady. The noisy and dark crow achieves its natural position within the world's framework. All things continue to exist naturally, beyond any sort of human authorization.

Human societies make judgment calls when defining categories through their constructed definitions. They determine which elements are considered part of dance or music and what holds actual value. Financial success, along with widespread acceptance and domination over others, serves as the basis for how people assess their worth and personal determination.

A complete view of this scenario reveals nothing other than nature's movements. Just life.

People identify patterns of illness as normal expressions of life processes. Every entity maintains its existence similarly to how human beings do—surviving their current state of existence.

People view viruses as harmful while simultaneously carrying viral liabilities toward other organisms. There's no villain, no hero. The natural lifecycle of the universe unfolds constantly throughout its eternal existence.

People do not live authentic lives because fear stands as their primary hindrance. Emotional outbursts drive our bodies to move before our minds have a chance to think.

We develop anxiety from enduring and stored emotional agonies that our minds retain from past suffering. Time progresses beyond these moments until individuals experience mental and visual impairment.

The real picture emerges only after we deeply observe fear. The current state of our closed eyes prevents us from perceiving the reality that exists before us.

So what now? Maybe nothing. Maybe just this—take a breath. Be here. The combination of your entire present state shapes the current life experiences occurring right now. No right, no wrong. Just this...

• 15 •

# II
# Transcending the Mind: The Path to True Awareness

Our minds persistently move in non-stop patterns similar to boundless sequences of thoughts and emotions.

Once individuals maintain their identification with mental chaos and random thoughts they create an unconnected reality that traps them inside fragmented states. Which shows that mental turbulence serves as our gateway to unveil transcendental peace beyond noise while revealing methods to achieve genuine inner peace.

### Why my mind show no peace because it perpetually fixates on planning the future while dwelling on experiences from the past?

Human consciousness functions just like flowing water which never ceases its movement. Our mind continuously moves because it stays connected to both our physical body along our time experiences and created life stories. But you are not this flow. Your observation point is Consciousness which exists separate from all things that appear before you. Your mind becomes chaotic when you identify thinking as your personal existence even though you exist in the present moment observing mental processes. The discovery of peace happens once individuals accept that belief.

## *Imagine a storm in the sky*

Although winds and clouds generate turbulence the sky stays peaceful with an unaltered condition. Your identity exists as the present awareness which observes the clouds in your mind. The sky represents your true nature since it stays present continuously without getting disturbed. After identifying and separating with clouds your mental disorder transforms into transient surface effects of outside disturbances.

## *Which steps lead me to stop associating with my thoughts?*

Observe them without judgment. The thoughts should be observed without intervention or mental resistance. Just watch. You will gradually become aware of how thoughts occur in a natural cycle. The discovery of peace happens through the cessation of resistance that leads to a state of inherent existence.

The fact that the mind functions as a reflection should explain its restless state of mind.

The mind remains agitated because people identify with their ego through the body as well as mental activity and emotional projections. This process of identification functions to split people between two categories: what belongs to them versus what belongs to everything else. Separate identity creates conflicts between people. Endless mental activity and battling arise from the actions of ego. Your self-existence transcends ego because you exist as an observer.

Your understanding of this fact brings an end to your feeling of restlessness.

A tree standing next to water's surface provides the perfect reflection for understanding this concept. The tree stays unchanged as the water disturbance causes reflection distortion. Depression in the mind creates warped perceptions of external reality in a manner similar to water.

Mankind perceives your authentic nature as steadfast and impervious to these external disturbances just like the tree that stands before it. The ego generates feelings of unrest yet you remain a silent witness who exists both present and motionless.

### *Of what significance is the mental observer who watches me rather than my thoughts which define me?*

Ask yourself: "Who am I?"

Through self-search you will experience that thoughts belong to Consciousness rather than self-generation. Through deep questioning the mind becomes calm and the ego weakens which reveals pure awareness that stays permanently present and still.

### *Since the mind appears illusory in nature then why would this illusion continue persisting?*

Your belief in the mind exists due to previous conditioning. Through its reflective nature the mind shows reality but it transforms perceptions into false distinctions which create confusion and produce suffering. Your belief in illusions creates an experience of chaos. Life seems chaotic until you understand Consciousness creates the mind which means chaos emerges from misperceiving the difference between your imagined thoughts and Reality.

Walking alone in darkness leads people to identify simulated objects as tangible things within that space.

When you are within darkness you tend to fear anything you spot. You understand the shadows were only illusions after switching on the light. Your perceptions of thoughts and fears alongside desires have the same illusory nature because your mind projects them into your awareness. Awareness functions like illumination which causes the disappearance of all shadows making mental disorder powerless.

### *Does any method exist to experience full detachment from mental processes?*

Practice self-inquiry. Keep asking, "Who am I?" Your true Self becomes evident when false layers of identification disappear. Total freedom occurs through knowledge instead of active pursuit. Accompanying the detachment from mind-projections leads to the natural appearance of peace. A tool functions as opposed to wielding control over the mind.

## *Observing thoughts without commitment brings about a sense of void in me. Is this progress?*

Yes. The emptiness demonstrates itself as the vast silent awareness that extends past all mental activity. Normal mental agitation makes the unconscious mind perceive tranquility as naive blankness. Such deep silence reveals your authentic self instead of indicating a lack of existence.

An ocean presents a picture of calmness during peaceful days. Outer calm conceals an endless well of depth which exists beneath the water. Through the absence of waves the ocean continues to exist in its complete form. Your silence does not imply nothingness because it represents your true self that exists as the cabin where all occurs without affecting its essential equilibrium.

## *Stillness represents something that should not instill feelings of fear?*

No, it is your very essence. An open attitude toward Stillness allows you to understand it contains nothing but peace and presence and awareness. The state you term as emptiness emerges when distractions cease to exist. Your interior limitless awareness reveals itself through inner quietness which already resided inside your being.

I constantly feel bewildered about the reason for my confusion.

The human mind triggers confusion when it develops dualities and creates illusions. Mental functions need partition as it generates sequences between wanting and fearing alongside failing to grasp things accurately. Discovering the mind serves as a thought-reflection rather than a truth-source enables you to access realities which transcend mental illusions.

## *What are the methods to prevent being deceived by false mental impressions?*

Self-inquiry stands as the crucial practice for this purpose. Ask yourself, Who am I? The practice of self-inquiry allows you to cut through illusions of the mind because it brings your attention back to unchanging awareness that exists beyond all thoughts and beliefs. Stepping away from delusions through continuous questioning reveals your authentic nature. The mind continuously does projection work but you now release the influence of its illusions over your understanding.

My mind continues being disorderly even after I investigate its inner workings although there must be a fundamental reason behind my suffering. My suffering requires further investigation to identify its fundamental cause.

Yes. Ignorance about your essential nature produces the mental disorder that you experience. You will experience suffering because you identify yourself with the mind which constantly changes its thoughts. Your mistaken identification of your self as your cognitive expressions along with your feelings leads to your suffering. Beyond all thoughts and emotions your actual self continues to exist in reality.

The heavens would be obscured by an endless cover of clouds. The gigantic sky underlies all clouds regardless of their fleeting presence which produces mere visual disturbances in the observer. The pure awareness you truly are exists at the level of a silent sky whereas your thoughts function as passing clouds briefly filling the space of your mind.

Your state of identification with clouds makes you lose sight of the sky. Throughout your awakening journey you understand that you exist as the vast sky but not as the temporary clouds passing through it.

## You suggest that minds together with their mental processes originate from ignorance?

Exactly. The mental states function similar to the waves which appear on ocean surfaces. These surface phenomena are temporary yet they never manage to modify the depth which exists beneath them. Upon realizing your true nature you witness the mental process as a temporary thought flow which does not determine your identity.

This understanding does not involve mind suppression rather it demonstrates that you watch mental activity instead of being the key participant.

## What method will enable me to eliminate ignorance from my life?

To achieve liberation one must practice self-reflection through accepting what comes. Your profound examination of the origins of your thinking patterns reveals that the genuine you exists within awareness which monitors experiences without involvement. Realization creates an understanding that leads to the end of ignorance which then liberates you.

## How should I handle the mental chaos after perceiving its true nature without getting engulfed in emotional reactions?

The path to true freedom leads to being able to watch the mind's turbulent state without any fear or emotional investment. The natural state of mind is to experience constant change. The power to let this inner chaos lead you exists but you retain the freedom to be in control of yourself.

Imagine a turbulent river. The river bustles powerfully next to you but you stand safely on the shore studying its movement. Since you view yourself as distinct from the stream you remain calmly stable while observing the flow. Observing the mental turmoil from a stable point of view allows you to recognize your role as pure awareness which houses all emerging and disappearing thoughts.

## When mental chaos hits a level that becomes difficult to handle does it then lose its control?

The feeling of mental heaviness should remind you that you exist outside of the mind. The awareness exists behind both you and the creative mind. The mental turbulence cannot harm awareness because the sky remains unaffected by atmospheric storms. Your commitment to awareness enables you to distance yourself from mental changes. From this vantage point you will observe that mental chaos exists only as a brief disturbance instead of an eternal state.

At your core you possess an unalterable condition that combines complete stillness with perfect peace.

## A person finds genuine peace through understanding their observer nature?

Exactly. Knowledge of being the observer of mental activity brings about peace because you recognize the difference between your true nature and mental processes. The advent of mental turmoil will continue yet it ceases to determine your identity.

You are eternal, unchanging awareness.

Recognizing this fact makes the mind powerless to control you so you stay peacefully unaffected by its actions. This is true freedom.

### If my essence exists beyond mental functions then how does the mind function in my daily life do I need to completely abandon it?

The brain serves as a necessary device which enables humans to travel through life but it exists outside the classification of goodness or wickedness. But it is not who you are.

Temporary thoughts exist alongside memories as well as emotions and perceptions within the operational range of the mind. The valuable things exist only when you maintain separation from your sense of identity. Your knowledge that you represent awareness watching the mind makes the mind powerless against your direction. Your deeper purpose receives service from a mind that supports you as the observer of thoughts.

A painter stands with his brush in hand. Maximum art creation depends on the brush but artistic identity remains separate from the brush. As a tool the mind helps you think and sense and make moves in the world though your true nature is distinct from your thoughts because you are the witnessing presence that exists beyond thoughts.

### The mind operates as an instrument while I maintain my sense of self separate from the functioning of this instrument

Exactly. The mind functions best when employed competently as a tool yet the individual should avoid clinging to it. The tool performs action as needed yet it carries no impact on the core identity.

The discovery of this fact shifts your mind into being a beneficial companion from becoming an authoritarian controller. Your continued thinking and perception activities will no longer stem from ego-driven self-identity because they will emerge from your complete knowledge of your authentic essence.

I need to uphold this awareness when living daily life despite all potential diversions.

Additional consciousness comes through returning frequently to wonder about your identity and by allowing the mind to observe passively. Your continuous practice brings the outside world distractions to lose their grip on you.

Although the world serves with its constant movement your authentic self stays unaltered. You remain in the world although your sense of being belongs elsewhere. The mind functions as a device while your permanent condition exists separate from all activity.

### I want to understand how someone can overcome all mental illusions while truly transcending their mind. Does this process happen as one step or occur in phases?

Freedom requires an ultimate step or exists along an infinite path of progression.

People who transcend mind illusions do not strive to reach distant objectives nor accomplish specific goals. This amounts to understanding what has always remained true. Your target freedom exists inside of you since you will uncover it through self-realization.

Human beings transcend mental boundaries because they stop identifying with their minds. Moving forward with this awareness becomes simpler than most people imagine. Coming back several times into your true nature's awareness via the experience of I am will achieve your freedom.

### Imagine a dream

During dream state you experience a full belief in reality. You recognize the illusions only after waking up from your dream. Like the mind forcefully manufactures the delusion that exists between separation and suffering. Your understanding of your original self reveals your existence as the mind transcendent consciousness. Once the illusions fade you can observe your mind as a brief mental construction that cannot establish your identity.

### The basic truth lies in understanding that mental grasp does not exist mainly because it reflects our ignorant states

Yes. Self-realization removes all power of the mind to dominate us. After illusions disappear reality shows itself clearly. The realization of self-identity occurs when the mind ceases to establish your personal identity.

You are unchanging consciousness.

Understand this truth and the influence of the mind will be eliminated. Through witnessing you remain an observer of mental activity while staying separate from it.

## When the mind receives transcendent revelation what substance manifests?

The consciousness of your true self remains as the sole awareness of your existence. This state brings both peace and freedom and silence. This is the eternal current moment which completes itself with everything in existence.

Total liberation emerges through freeing yourself from both your thoughts and any concepts which allows you to express your eternal nature as Original Consciousness.

# III

# Unlearning to Be: "Breaking Free from the Illusion of Control"

Sitting with oneself to figure out the difference between genuine reality and acquired personal habits—has that ever crossed your mind? I wonder about our personal essence because, beyond basic actions, we also need to understand which thoughts and emotions truly belong to us and which ones we have absorbed through cultural learning.

Every day brings a smooth transition between wakefulness and motion, followed by chasing and relaxation. It's comfortable, predictable. Yet, some secret inner voice continuously questions the present state, whispering, "Is this all there is?"

Human beings are on a perpetual quest for answers, maintaining an everlasting search due to the underlying feelings that exist within our consciousness. People pursue greater meaning even when they have enough because the inner voice demands it. A different path lies ahead—beyond both possessions and accomplishments.

The issue arises when our pattern of accumulation and search for knowledge becomes ambiguous, making it unclear whether we are truly getting closer to our goal. It begins to resemble constructing a more elegant prison enclosure.

Look at the mind—it's restless. It continuously runs calculations, attempting to predict every situation like a game in its pursuit of success.

And when it gets tired? The mind occupies itself with internal thoughts while gazing outward, patiently awaiting an opportunity for liberation.

But liberation from what?

There's no prison, no chains. Just us. Our inner narratives provide all the limitations we need to live within.

People believe they require external discoveries to obtain answers and significance for their existence. But perhaps life seeks a different approach—not about accumulating more, but about undoing.

We need to strip away all acquired coverings and the concepts we maintain in order to exist as we truly are.

Sounds simple, right? But simplicity isn't always easy. We claim to seek peace, yet our bodies tense whenever silence fills the environment. Most people say they seek truth, yet they deny it when it presents unexpected challenges. People express the desire for romantic love while simultaneously maintaining careful expectations that restrict their affection.

## Why?

All true seeing requires the abandonment of our grip. And letting go? The real feeling of uncertainty mirrors the experience of entering unfamiliar territory.

The mind doesn't like that. Control and absolute certainty are its main objectives. Yet, life offers little consistency upon close examination. Everything changes, everything moves. At this very instant, the present moment is already flowing into the past.

Perhaps genuine liberation exists beyond additional knowledge, possessions, or activities.

True freedom may arise from trusting thoughts as they exist in their natural space. People can experience life without clinging to it because they trust their capacity to comprehend it.

Human beings classify additional things as possessions that they try to control. The pursuit of greater success, recognition, and wisdom also aims to enhance personal meaning. But the true "more"?

It is the transformation itself, rather than an improvement. The method for surpassing superficial thinking and mental manipulations exists.

Our minds consistently pursue something despite the endless cycle. If any of these potential fulfillments truly provided satisfaction, we should already be content.

## *And yet, here we are.*

Maybe that's the point. Life may not have a definable endpoint or conclusion because being present in constant questioning is its true purpose. A person should fully and openly commit to the question, setting aside all fears.

The goal is to exist without possessing, controlling, or grasping anything—only to truly be.

Such awareness may be the perfect destination, even if it fails to satisfy everyone.

Shared Experiences:

"My memories" vs. "Your memories" = "Our shared past."

"My knowledge" vs. "Your knowledge" = "Innovation."

"My traditions" vs. "Your traditions" = "Cultural fusion."

Our perception of reality differs from person to person, yet there exists a shared aspect between us. The world we observe is a common ground, intersecting within our perceptions.

Think about it. Two people standing in parallel positions before the same sky will most likely view different aspects from their individual perspectives.

One may notice the grandeur of the horizon, while the other focuses on a single distant cloud. Both are true. Both are real. Reality extends beyond both perceptions.

It's the same with everything—space, time, meaning—whatever you choose. Let's take space as an example. A single point connects with infinite straight lines that extend in all directions.

The idea of space leads us in two ways: infinite straight lines expanding continuously or forming circular patterns.

Without assuming a central reference point, we might perceive an unstructured collection of floating dots.

There's reality—what is. And then there's the method we use to understand reality, which exists as a separate concept from what actually is.

Our way of thinking and interpretation exists independently of reality itself. This perception remains only one possible way of understanding things.

Some call it intelligence. Some call it perception. Some call it an illusion. According to the Bhagavad Gita, reality is maya, operating through different layers that allow us glimpses of truth but never its full comprehension.

The Quran explains that numerous signs exist worldwide to guide those who wish to look beneath the surface. Various ancient texts, including the Bible and the Vedas, teach that we see the world yet fail to grasp its entirety.

Different backgrounds unite us, for there is always a shared foundation—

A shared essence.

This essence has been referred to as consciousness, awareness, the soul, or another appropriate word. Humanity contains something beyond understanding, something that defines us as human beings.

We possess an ability to experience love, to feel awe, and to sense a truth beyond verbal definitions.

Every human thought, philosophy, argument, and belief functions as an attempt to understand existence. But they are not the thing itself—merely perspectives.

The knowledge that we grasp truth through intuition provides our best access to reality.

During personal contemplation, one must wonder about our current situation.

Beyond the constant uproar of our activities, desires for possessions, and classifications—what is actually happening?

It's funny, isn't it? People work hard to understand the world by creating simplified classification systems defining right and wrong, good and bad. Yet, when they attempt to label things, each concept seems to escape their grasp.

Consider intelligence for a moment. Many assume knowledge operates on four levels, labeled A through D, with intelligence culminating at Epoch E—representing complete understanding.

But the separation between E and the other categories never truly existed. Every intelligence level within A, B, C, and D contains the essence of E at its core.

Our failure to see objects as one unified entity stems from dividing them into fragments.

People have limited access to complete reality. Our understanding of life is shaped by words, fleeting experiences, and fragmented information. But words?

They are merely symbols representing the deeper meaning beneath. Thousands of words from me hold no guarantee of your understanding, for true experience lies beyond words—it cannot be fully communicated through language.

We live in loops, don't we? Closed within ourselves. Either through willpower or fear of confronting external realities.

The true irony is that fear and aggressive emotions fuel themselves endlessly. Hurt circulates—one person's pain leading them to inflict pain upon another, and so on.

Hate breeds hate. True destruction happens when a person refuses to doubt their belief that they are right.

The issue extends beyond society—it's deeply personal. The mind is wild. Our physical presence is small, yet our mental reach extends across time.

We relive the past, imagine the future. The same imagination that creates art and music also generates anxiety and doubt.

The mind that discovered fire also questions its own identity.

And the funny thing? Our attempts to resolve problems often create new ones. It's a never-ending game. Once we achieve a goal, another emerges.

The object we once desired transforms into a hidden burden. Life becomes heavier when we accumulate too much without caution. Sometimes, we must let things go.

Step back. Question what is truly necessary.

Balance. That is the core. The dance between your inner world and the outer world.

And here we are. Two people, occupying this moment. No authority, no grand conclusions. Just an exchange of ideas—rooted in love, in the sheer joy of existence.

People possess a peculiar talent for keeping themselves in the present moment. Memory, imagination, and expectation complete our human experience of being.

That's what makes us human. But sometimes, in this dance of time, we forget to actually live.

So what is life? Does life maintain a great purpose, similar to missions with specific guidelines?

Or is it simply this—the current existential experience is what life, here and now, truly represents.

And love? Ah, love. The experiences of love result in various explanations that people share with one another.

Love exists as both a sensation and a moral responsibility, as well as a binding relationship between people.

When it comes to the most profound form of love, we are merely intended to exist alongside one another.

The awareness of being present in yourself creates interdependence, which then leads to an awareness of the life force all around you.

Not for gain, not for self—just for the joy of existing together.

Our heart allows us to see our true identity in every individual. Touching another person's spiritual essence unlocks our personal spiritual presence.

My answer to life's meaning would be simple. A definite meaning does not exist. The answer to this question is not found in a mathematical equation.

But there is love. The journey to love does not lead to a particular place since it represents the way we should move ahead.

Being completely yourself brings about an enjoyable state of existence.

Be yourself until you aren't. Live fully, breathe deeply. Life is here. Now. That's all there ever is.

Life keeps people questioning its essential purpose. Like, really, what's the point? Flowers do not ponder their existence; they simply bloom.

A river does not stop to wonder about its destination; the water continues to flow. The sun shines because that is its nature. Yet, we continually attempt to discover our purpose in life despite all our efforts.

The essential aspect of living is to experience life through questions without seeking a definitive response. The pursuit of dream destinations can cause you to miss out on reality by neglecting your present journey.

Standing motionless from fear prevents people from taking action, keeping them stuck. People often wish for rain on sunny days yet crave sunshine when it rains.

Our constant pursuit of the future prevents us from existing in the present, where life truly unfolds.

The only real compass in all this? Honesty. You need to embrace honesty consistently—not just the kind you present to others, but the kind that truly matters to your soul.

Internal transformation begins when you stop tightening the knots in your heart and abandon contradictory living.

And that something is love. Love exists independently of conditions or poetry—purely as a constant state of existence that all people should embrace.

It takes great courage to accept that there are parts of life you do not fully comprehend.

The path to genuine living starts when you let things be. The biggest and most challenging peak you will ever encounter lies deep within your being.

Most individuals evaluate life through quantitative achievements such as wealth and success, despite the fact that true meaning does not align with numerical measures.

They don't fit into equations. An authentic flowing river does not concern itself with criticisms about its intensity.

It just moves. And so should you. Letting go of control enables you to witness the natural path of your destiny. Ever watched a bird fly?

The bird moves its wings only when needed, gliding effortlessly on air currents. Existence often works better when we surrender to its flow instead of fighting to control it.

The value of existence reveals itself through personal experience. Words are just words. They attempt to capture ideas, yet they remain constrained by the human mind that created them.

People who spend too much time defining life often miss out on actually living.

Our difficulty in life stems from our fear of giving ourselves space. The human desire for permanence compels us, even as the world around us constantly changes.

People occupy themselves with real and imagined problems to gain a sense of control. But control is an illusion. Holding too tightly to a kite keeps it from soaring.

By never letting go of the string, you will never discover where the wind could have taken it. Life is about finding the balance between holding on and letting go.

All our existence and knowledge come from past generations. Who first discovered fire? Who decided to cook food? Who took the risk of eating a fruit to see if it was safe?

We live upon countless unnamed contributions, yet we often act as if we built everything ourselves. Ego creates the illusion that we possess things and accomplish everything alone. But the truth?

We have inherited everything. Realizing this dissolves the ego, replacing it with appreciation for all life.

Despite this, we remain trapped in our isolated perspectives. Everyone lives within their own reality, shaped by personal memories and experiences. Two people can look at the same object yet perceive it completely differently.

All disputes arise because people forget that their perspective is singular.

We created systems—language, laws, religion, science—to find meaning in chaos. Yet, none of these fully bridge human understanding.

Have you really heard what I'm trying to say? Systems like philosophy, science, and religion cannot establish absolute truths. But look around. Everyone is certain.

Certain that their opinion is correct. Certain that doubt is weakness. We create barriers between ourselves by insisting on absolute truth. And that's where suffering begins.

Do you see it now? All conflicts stem from our desire for control and the need to be right. I do not claim universal knowledge. The only truth I grasp is that love is the only path forward. Love is not an abstract concept; it is a way of living that must be shared, not turned into a battleground.

Love is beyond human control. It cannot be held or owned. It simply flows. Love exists in the open space where you stop proving yourself, stop trying to own or control others.

Love is the last thing that remains when everything else fades away.

Look at a rose. A rose remains beautiful without effort because it simply exists as it is. A rose keeps its fragrance whether admired or plucked. It exists fully, without hesitation.

The human purpose is much the same. Life is about being—unfolding without fear.

Those who search endlessly, despite distractions, will find their purpose in love.

Not the kind that asks for something in return. The heart finds its true joy in love that exists without conditions. The more you give, the more you are replenished. Love has no boundaries, no restrictions.

It dissolves the self, leaving only infinity.

Love is not a decision. Love is the only way.

Have you ever considered whether we ask the right questions in life? Some spend their lives searching for answers. Others never bother. But which matters more—the question or the answer?

And if we find an answer, will it still hold meaning after discovery?

Because life keeps shifting. The ground moves beneath us. The goalposts change. Perhaps life is about both building and dismantling at the same time.

There is no prescribed way to live. The path belongs to no one but yourself.

If you climb a mountain, your footsteps will never match those before you. Your journey will shape your movement.

And one day, you may realize—there was never a mountain at all. Just a thought. Just an idea. You were always where you needed to be.

Words are funny things. They connect us, yet also divide us. Right, wrong. Science, religion. Me, you. This side, that side.

We define the world, then struggle against the definitions we created.

But can words break the boundaries they establish? If we stopped defining everything, even for a moment, could we simply be?

So let's pause. No labels, no filters. No rich or poor, no black or white, no boss or employee. Just you and me.

Here. At this moment.

Let's talk, human to human.


Maybe truth isn't a destination.

Maybe it's remembering.

What about suffering?

It's the fever of the mind. Our mind signals an imbalance within through specific cues. We have extensive mental health discussions, yet we approach the matter only through the lens of mechanical problems needing adjustment and optimization.

But the mind isn't a machine. It's a living thing. Anything alive demands proper nurturing with room for peace as well as periods of rest.

We overload it—constant stimulation, constant consumption. Society makes stress a desirable thing while using non-stop activity as a mark of social success.

Hustle culture presents rest as a sign of weakness according to its teachings. That silence is wasted time. But at what cost?

The moment of breakdown eventually becomes inevitable.

When a mind suffers a collapse due to carrying excessive weight, what occurs? Several explanations, which people use to construct their lives, have lost their sense of logical accuracy.

Our pursued sense of meaning disappears when we lose sight of it.

Life commences on this authentic journey at this stage because humanity achieves independence from external devotion.

As you continue to read this article right now, your thoughts may have been touched by its messages. Maybe not.

This could be one thought among many that will soon pass away.

When such a feeling arises, you should never disregard the experience or question appearing in your consciousness. Don't shove it aside. Sit with it. Let it breathe.

Looking for all answers is not the main goal, since the journey exists beyond obtaining explanations.
You need to focus on developing the correct set of questions.

Raise the necessary questions, because doing so can deliver complete solutions.

# IV

# The Space Between Thoughts

Mainly, the images and ancient stories remind us of life. The true meaning exists within the current scenario of our everyday lives.

People navigate the world with hopes that develop from recounted tales they have heard. Our internal search takes place while moving forward because our minds constantly scan all external areas except their true source.

The mind speaks in hushed tones to suggest that the entire experience may be an illusion while simultaneously responding with certainty that the world exists.

This inner force replies to the suggestion that these things make up everything that exists.

"Are you sure?"

"Yes. The whole world has been scrutinized through objective investigation, and after reviewing the stories, one discovers that nothing else remains."

"But isn't there something more?"

According to religious tradition, Buddha managed to discover it.

The statement raises a valid question: Does truth exist beyond these stories?

It continues forever in a circular pattern, similar to a snake following its own body extensions.

Is any of the presented information genuine at all? Are the accounts of spiritual progression factual? We don't know.

Over time, numerous people have passed down these religious relics, making it impossible for humans to determine what elements still remain true to their original form.

The meanings of words change to adapt to speakers' needs.

People consider the narrative about Krishna equivalent to Jesus' words and Shiva's teachings while also placing them on par with zombie sagas and superhero epics.

This current exchange, alongside all other tales we produce, amounts to additional narratives.

Does existence have any purpose with these considerations? Human beings naturally think to question and look for understanding. Since when did this habit start?

Does our search have any clear purpose?

Maybe it's all just entertainment. A game.

"But how do we live, then? The absence of meaning seems to make purposeless action impossible."

The entire process happens in a manner that resembles children during games—the moment requires full engagement while meaninglessness plays no role.

Every child continues to play because they understand the world provides safety during their games.

"Exactly. A child starts with an empty mind that takes everything from the experiences in their surroundings.

The sand shifts in multiple ways because it remains unfastened and mutable rather than being static or permanent.

The sand eventually transforms into concrete, which becomes both identity and personal self."

The story remains a series of mere words.

"Yes."

We lack any solid evidence demonstrating the truth behind these claims.

You ask what sort of concrete evidence would be enough for you.

"I don't know. Something real, something tangible. This all feels too abstract."

You cannot obtain food, water, or shelter through this teaching. But is survival all there is?

Society adores celebrated individuals according to its standards. Are they at peace?

Power, fame, and beauty represent additional self-created stories that we narrate to ourselves.

Life's fundamental inquiry reduces to a single question that seeks to identify personal identity.

People devote long hours to asking questions about external subjects, yet very few turn their questioning toward the self and the identity behind the queries.

Who is the singular identity that seeks to discover their true nature? And why does it ask?

Our lives change completely when we decide to direct the question toward ourselves. The external world functions easily when we define it through explanations that grant us security.

The investigation directed at the questioning entity produces insurmountable obstacles.

Human thinking reaches its boundary here. Such a metaphor describes reaching the final destination on a moving train.

After completing the journey, you will need to leave the train and continue walking. At this point, we freeze with terror in our bodies. The station marks the end of all tracks with no forthcoming assurance.

Our fear forces us to maintain our position on this train, which represents familiarity.

Like the river continuing through a waterfall and the tree persisting to grow despite its future cutting, nature does not stand in their way.

Life moves. It doesn't ask for permission.

Still, I get it. It's not a simple path. Words provide limited capability when you are investigating a subject.

We should spend some time considering this situation like we would rest beneath firewood in a dense woodland. No rush. Just listening.

You are the world. This concept is difficult to accept because it is factual. Each external object, from animals to rivers to mountains to wind, also exists as part of your inner self.

The fear that exists within animals originates from your internal emotions. Your love for dogs helps you understand how to love yourself.

You will find within your nature all the elements that exist outside—they exist right within you.

Nevertheless, we choose to exclude ourselves from this understanding. Fear makes us shut down.

Humans prevent themselves from experiencing the very opportunities they wish to have.

People avoid looking because they fear feeling emotions entirely while being reluctant to experience life completely.

And what do we do instead? We collect stories. Earthlings prefer secondhand truths over choosing to experience their own personal realities.

Each manufactured tale you live through develops new knots inside your body.

The tight knots build up one by one until they restrict your movements to a minimum. Is that the life you want?

For one instant, drop every tale inside your mind, even this specific one.

You versus me—it never ends. The fight continues while we exchange arguments for self-defense. The hatred burns from one person to another like hot tar.

Words? They don't reach anymore. They're just sounds now—hollow echoes. The words that pass your mental barriers would reveal themselves to your heart if you considered them.

Make love the foundation of your existence rather than hatred. Fear strangles love. Ownership limits it. Our excessive grip causes love to vanish away.

When you are convinced that destruction originates only through hatred, do you really believe it? No.

The most catastrophic human-made disasters occurred because individuals worked under the delusion that their actions were beneficial.

Both goodness and wickedness reside inside each person rather than existing solely outside.

Ignorance blinds us.

Living solely through assumptions leads to what outcome?

The lack of inquiry about life's nature, death's purpose, time's passage, and our life's significance is what this is.

No one knows the future.

The natural process shows us that daily transformations create the birth of darkness from brightness while watercourses reach their end to form the beginning of the ocean.

Isn't everything just transformation?

The death of ignorance brings forth clarity about truth.

It will remove our ignorance from us unless we willingly release our grip.

Only the truth remains.

So let's ask again:

The present moment stands alone without any relation to past or future events. Would you still be anxious? Has your grip on life not weakened?

Do you prefer to exist as an open, calm, loving, free person?

If you have ever, even for the shortest period, sensed this presence, then perhaps you have already experienced reality.

And maybe that's enough.

What now? Well, maybe nothing. Maybe just take a breath. Listen to the wind. Watch the shadows flicker.

Forget about seeking the meaning behind everything for now and remain present in the moment.

Our only real action in this world consists of fulfilling our purpose.

# V

# The Mastery of Destiny: A Conversation on Fate and Free Will

Does life seem to have predetermined your direction? Some unavoidable power determines your destination without considering your efforts at moving forward. All humans have experienced those instances at some stage of their lives. The many names people use to describe this unseen force include fate, destiny, God's will, karma and the universe. People struggle to make choices when everything apparently exists as an established plan. Our impactful choices does not explain the sense of losing control we experience over our lives.

Think about it. Everyone receives their birth conditions when fate decides their place of birth and the parents they inherit and the bodily form they possess. We observe that individuals receive total life advantages including abundant wealth and power and excellent health while multiple persons face daily battles. People from every belief system agree that specific aspects totally escape human control. Broadly speaking Prarabdha Karma explains that we originally inherit certain struggles from our past karma before we were born according to the teachings of the Bhagavad Gita. According to the Bible we gain what we produce. According to Quran's teaching divine intervention exists because God predetermined certain events but people's deeds still determine their responsibilities. According to all these traditions a delicate relationship exists between events that were already determined and those which depend on human actions.

So where does that leave us? Human beings seem destined between being complete products of divine influences and exercising control in crafting their existences or shaping their life pathway.

Here's where it gets interesting. Human existence includes unalterable circumstances such as birth and death but people possess a tremendous ability to shape their world. According to the Vedas Purushartha signifies the determination and purpose we generate in life. Shakespeare's dramatic characters acknowledge the universal truth about human destiny because they must decide which elements of their life the gods control versus which aspects depend on their personal choices. Our life's essence transcends external experiences because our reactions determine its essence more than the events that occur to us.

We see this every day. Two people experiencing similar challenges develops into one person becoming resilient and the other person descends into depression. Why? Within the limits that fate puts on us we still maintain freedom to decide. The power we possess emerges from our mindset together with our ability to choose action based on our attitude.

Maybe fate is like a river. You exist in the current which neither allows stoppage nor temporary suspension. The flow of water allows you to choose between swimmng and steering your course and determining your approach towards the currents. Drifters permit the water to control their destination. Some people understand how to travel efficiently while staying true to themselves despite the flow of fate.

The role of character appears at this moment. The destiny you experience emerges directly from the combination of your actions and habits and disciplined self that you become as a person. According to the Gita "A man's own self functions both as friend and enemy." Meaning? The choice between different types of persons exists within your power although it determines everything about your future self. The delivery of your lines depends entirely on you regardless of the script life presents you with.

The essential point we should ask ourselves concerns how we respond to our innate destiny rather than whether fate exists or not. The question you should ask yourself is this: What am I doing with everything that has been entrusted to me? Our role becomes essential since destiny creates the setting yet it is only our responsibility to execute our part in this world.

### *What do you think? Our existence exists within the power of destiny or does our personal decision-making shape our destiny?*

We see this every day. Quasi identical difficulties hit two people yet one transforms into strength and the other slips into depression. Why? The space allowed by destiny gives us the freedom to make choices during our existence. Our ability to pick our actions combined with our mindset and attitude constitutes our genuine power.

Maybe fate is like a river. The river carries you from beneath and there exists no way to halt its continuous flow. Swimming in this current gives you options to either confront it or let it guide you. People allow water to determine their direction rather than swimming toward their intended destinations. A subset of individuals develops intentional movement which allows them to create their path through the existing circumstances.

Character acts as an essential determining factor. Your future destiny depends entirely on the person you become because of what you choose to do, how you practice and the discipline you develop. In its verses the Gita maintains that "A man's personal self functions both as a friend and as an enemy toward him."

You control the selection of your personality which will impact all aspects of your existence. You maintain complete control over your message delivery even if life provides a predetermined script to you.

People should examine destiny beyond "Is fate real?" an easy attempt at the question. The essential matter concerns my response to the opportunities life provides. The ultimate responsibility rests with us to take action in the world we have been provided by our destiny.

### *What do you think? The direction of life stems from our destinies or do human actions generate our personal destinies?*

### *Deeds, Character, and Destiny – A Real Talk on Fate & Free Will*

People should understand how humans approach the topic of destiny versus personal choice starting with this discussion about Fate and freedom. Constant arguments in daily life focus on whether everything is predetermined or humans have control over their personal choices. The argument between both sides makes valid points regarding this subject.

The concept that fate and free will must exist as opposites lacks merit. These concepts exist like two pieces which form one complete whole. Think about it.

Our every selection creates an irreversible effect. The ability to act and begin new endeavors defines free will so that humans possess this power to start and complete tasks. After making a decision the outcomes automatically begin to fulfill themselves into existence which becomes our fate because it results from what we initiated.

## It's like planting a seed

Your free will comes into play because you are responsible for selecting which seeds to plant. The fate of a planted seed determines the type of tree which will eventually grow from it. The seed selection sets the future outcomes which cannot be altered. Placing mango seeds never results in developing apples as the final outcome. That's karma. The principle described as cause and effect operates in our reality.

## You Are What You've Done

People state that their birth-given character should remain unchallenged. I didn't choose that!" Fair question. Character does not arrive by random chance at the time of our birth. The construction process takes place through consistent actions and repeated choices accumulated over time.

Muscle memory serves as the best analogy for what happens to your personality and character. People who have played the piano for several years develop natural reflexes in their fingers. The practices you dedicate your days to whether for hundreds of years or only several years create essential traits within you. Natural calmness appears in certain people different from those who express quick reactions. It's not random. Repeated actions accumulate to form this outcome throughout several years.

Since your personality develops through action you possess the power to transform it. All daily activities create the individual you will become in the future. It's never too late.

## Why Do Bad Things Happen to Good People?

Have you ever observed that really good people face difficulties even though certain individuals with questionable character succeed without limits? Seems unfair, right? But let's zoom out a bit.

Is it possible to find a virtuous person facing adversity in present times? The person might possibly be paying back debts accrued through their past actions from this life or another existence. Even though the lying rich man continues to succeed in life you can see through his deception. The person benefits from his previous charitable conduct. The chance to pay occurs at every time period. All people without exception will eventually experience the outcomes of their activities.

The universe isn't random. There's a rhythm, a balance. The Bhagavad Gita together with the Bible as well as the Quran and the Vedas provide the same message about human accountability for their actions. Each deed creates a domino effect in the universe independent of any retributive intention by a higher authority.

## What's Now?

*This valued information brings up the question which we should pursue. Simple. This lesson requires us to monitor the things we sow. Time will reveal your future harvest despite how clearly you notice its approaching.*

You want a better future? Start making better choices today. You want peace? Your actions should bring peace into being. You want success? Commit yourself to action because wasting time through jealousy will not lead you to success.

The path from your past has transformed you yet it remains separate from your actual identity. You determine the path your life takes through the decisions you make one by one.

*Free will and destiny exist in constant motion with one another.*

## The Law of Life: What You Saw, You Recap

*The universe has a habit of displaying our inserted effort through a powerful reflective process. It's like a mirror. After thoughts together with actions and verbal expressions produce returns which match the inputs. Expectations and time periods differ when the effects manifest.*

People who work diligently move forward in life since their efforts attract more possibilities. Continuous procrastination leads individuals to observe their things disappear instead of expand. The universe operates through natural causes that link actions to their effects rather than punished for wrongdoings. The Bhagavad Gita defines this phenomenon as Karma while the Bible describes it as receiving back what a person puts out and Quran states that every soul must provide an account for its deeds. Different words, same truth.

The matter extends beyond personal life to national prosperity. National success follows leaders who maintain integrity but leads to national decline when greed control takes over. Reliable hindsight repeatedly demonstrates these truths throughout recorded times.

Economy of any successful civilization starts dying from the inside out.

My understanding accepts that rebirth remains a belief which some people do not share without judgment. The principle stands true even in our current existence because we witness the same phenomenon. The act of spreading kindness helps a person find good responses from others.

People who deceptively steal from others discover themselves to be within a sphere of doubted trust. People who follow ethical conduct remain in their current situation while those who choose dishonesty reside in the conditions they have established for themselves.

# VI

# Psychology of self-understanding

Modern society has mastered every aspect beyond human bodily control. Science has delivered to society its fundamental aspects of speed coupled with technology alongside medicine. The question now becomes whether we can properly master our personal minds since we outperform machines in outer space exploration.

The traditional teachings of antiquity involved more than religious ceremonies since they demanded comprehension of human mental processes. All three figures including yogis from India and mystics from Middle East together with saints from the West shared a common understanding of self-study. They studied the mind. These sages mastered the mental nature of their creatures together with their wants and anxieties. A genuine master understands it is self-control that represents their true achievement rather than seeking to control external matters.

Self-control requires time to develop because it handles more slowly than one might think. It's a lifelong practice. To understand ourselves as a human being we need to observe ourselves just like scientists learn from nature while experimenting with their observations.

Mind Observation means you track your thoughts. What triggers you? What patterns repeat?

Instead of analysis focus on identifying which habits create peaceful states. Which ones cause suffering?

Self-understanding leads to recognizing that each thought generates an action which forms your life direction.

The next step calls for selecting actions and thoughts which reflect your future self-image.

As self-control develops naturally throughout time it transforms into an automatic habit for the practitioner. The transformation has brought you to a state of mature response instead of impulsive reaction.

The true scientific knowledge which ancient masters used to teach exists here. The controlling power over emotions differentiates between an emotionally driven person versus someone who exercises active guidance.

Although most people think of this as philosophy it actually constitutes practical knowledge. It's practical. Reflect on the wise and most successful individuals who also exhibit peaceful traits among all those you have encountered. Were they easily shaken? People demonstrate either an intense awareness of maintaining inner calm or they demonstrate excessive emotional reactions. Through internal exploration people can achieve this state.

## *Why This Matters*

As the day ends neither the universe nor any cosmic power offers rewards or punishments to anyone. It's just responding to us. Getting the fruit from your field depends on what you choose to plant there. A well-tended field provides the foundation for developing a better world and better lives with stronger relationships.

The good news? We obtain an opportunity to set new seeds every day.

There exists something we need to discuss together in a genuine manner. Our minds face the challenge of spending time alone in total silence without any interruptions or invalidating excuses. It's not easy. People typically shun this experience from birth until death. Judging people with the willingness to confront their pure awareness will reveal the totality of themselves alongside their suppressed emotions and concealed fears. Nothing is left in the dark.

Nobody can continue to pretend at this stage since everything becomes entirely visible. At this point you eliminate all pretenses regarding your faults and eradicate self-deceptions around them. People neither embellish their value with empty pride nor reduce their worth with disbelief in themselves. Your personal view reveals your exact being to yourself. After becoming fully aware of yourself you start on an immense journey of growth.

Every human must learn to resist following passive urges and emotions without consideration. Different spiritual traditions such as the Gita and the Bible together with the Quran and Vedas convey a unified message that personal triumph emerges through controlling your own self. Your true life begins at the very instant you escape the dominance of random situations and trivial mental events baseless fears and unreasonable desires.

People should not react automatically to all sensory impulses and emotional triggers that occur. Several religious texts including the Gita and Bible, Quran, and Vedas convey the same wisdom about achieving real victory through self-control. True living begins when you manage to get free from being directed by every passing thought and each fear or craving.

Tending fieldwork serves as a good analogy for this process. When you seek quality produce you must not randomly cast seeds into untamed terrains while expecting exceptional results. You prepare the soil. You uproot any destructive habits and thoughts since they only cause depletion. Available space becomes essential for planting correct actions combined with right intention and hardened efforts. As you keep working the field will reward you by developing something durable that arises from actual reality. True living develops from order instead of disorder.

Eventually we discover a level that goes beyond basic knowledge—it touches the understanding. You gain understanding beyond personal understanding of how life operates in its entirety. Something equivalent to gravity exists in life to maintain equilibrium in all things. Karma serves as an equivalent term for justice and cause and effect alongside other principles. Your released energy will eventually arrive back to you. Every single thought combined with each action creates a chain reaction that forms into the next step of life. The functioning of universal balance remains harmonious regardless of any reward or punishment system.

People usually live their lives while trying to acquire happiness alongside preventing pain until they understand that both are effects of their personal decisions. When you line your actions with this greater rightness instead of what feels pleasant now you will create a transformation. Living by this principle turns you from a helpless life passenger into its top controller.

This isn't about some mystical, out-there wisdom. It's practical. It's everyday life. You build discipline not by chasing secrets but by showing up, making better choices, and keeping promises to yourself. Real willpower isn't some magic trick—it's built in the small moments, the tiny decisions that shape who you become.

At the end of the day, this isn't about some grand, unreachable enlightenment. It's about being awake to yourself. Knowing who you are. Owning your choices. And in that, there's a kind of peace that no outside force can shake.

So, what do you think? Are you willing to really see yourself? Because once you do, there's no going back. But then again—why would you want to?

People continuously tell themselves they need to build strength yet they tightly hold onto their personal weaknesses the way a child grips a ruined plaything. People portray a desire for freedom yet they fear dismissing their restricting chains.

The power to become strong cannot be achieved by mere desires. You cannot develop willpower if you surrender to all minor temptations at once. Growth toward strength requires facing your shortcomings before resolving to fight against them today.

You possess every tool required for developing willpower inside your mind. All of your daily challenges and destructive routines with periods of inactivity serve as developing opportunities rather than mere difficulties. They are training grounds. Each time you defeat weakness you develop a mind that becomes more robust and focused through disciplined training.

I will explain the procedure through simple instructions.

Abandon all behaviors that continuously emerge your energy.

Build habits that strengthen you.

Your attention should rest on the current tasks and activities.

Stop overthinking—act.

Establish guiding principles for your life which you need to follow religiously.

Speak with intention, not impulse.

You must control your mind because failure to do so will result in its control over you.

The ideas transform when someone devotes sincere attention to them while implementing them effectively. Not immediately, not without effort, but definitely. Understanding that the initial step which involves breaking bad habits poses significant challenges to most individuals. Performing this requires both continuous attempt along with occasional inner battles against your own self. Pushing back against weaknesses creates stronger willpower in the process.

Everyone searches for shortcuts which would reveal secret ways to develop willpower without facing difficulty. People seek an easy solution but such methods do not exist. The selection of comfort instead of discipline maintains your weak state. The path to growth becomes possible through your ability to move past uncomfortable situations. Simple as that.

Developing resistance against bad behaviors will lead to improved abilities for building good behaviors. Creating good habits depends on your ability to stay present while bad habit quitting demands pure determination. You have to make your mind active by focusing your attention on everything you do. A person who develops these skills naturally learns to pay more attention to the present. People who adopt this mind-set carry out tasks by focusing their attention with sharp precision. No half-hearted efforts. No sloppy work. All necessary activities receive prompt execution. Being late provides the same outcome as other forms of weakness.

The largest aspect lies in following rules. Living by rules leads to personal freedom since it removes the influence of automatic undesired behavior. Each day you take control of the food you eat and schedule your sleeping time alongside the contents of your mind. When your impulses take control of your actions then you become subservient to your cravings as well as distractions and laziness. A well-disciplined life proves to be stronger than monotonous. A disciplined life transforms you from being controlled by your actions into becoming the one who controls them.

And then there's the tongue. By mastering your speaking abilities you gain mastery over wider aspects of your life. Words carry weight. Speaking without care results in a failure to think with purpose. A person who uses their mindfulness to speak obtains powerful results through their words.

And finally, the mind. This is the battlefield. All training of habits together with rule-setting along with verbal control ultimately reach this point. Mental direction stands as the highest strength that exists. Basics of life lie in training your thinking to shape your future results.

These things receive minimal acknowledgment from our contemporary society. The world teaches a message of self-care and pleasure combined with rest but hardly speaks about discipline. People who establish discipline through their minds will be trained to gain control over their lives rather than letting their environment dominate them.

Your life builds by construction when you build yourself and it falls into decay when you let go of control. Each decision along with all ideas and deeds creates elements for the vast structure of your personality. Build wisely.

# VII
# The Art of Concentration

We need to explore the fundamental yet strong concept of concentration. We hear about concentration frequently but most of us fail to truly comprehend its meaning. Following the mind's operation resembles lessons learned from controlling wild horses. Alas when you do not train it the mind will wander uncontrolled. A properly guided mind under discipline transforms into an incomparable vital power.

The accomplishment of any activity demands focused attention. Everyone needs focus to achieve any goal since concentration stands as the essential foundation behind personal achievements. Everyone uses this ability regularly because concentration operates without mystical aspects and belongs to everyone. When you lose yourself within a demanding book it leads you to forget how much time has passed. That's concentration. Have you ever spent so much focus on something that your surrounding environment forgotten to exist? That's it too. We widely consider this simple skill as something rare although it remains straightforward.

Most individuals find themselves confused at this point. Some individuals believe that concentration requires focused staring at a candle flame for long durations and mantric chanting as they create mental stillness to the outside world. According to true practices concentration does not demand isolation since you must direct your entire attention to your current actions regardless of how regular they appear. The practice of concentration happens in any task from writing to cooking and from playing sports to floor sweeping. The Bhagavad Gita joins forces with the Bible alongside the Quran and Vedas by discussing this concept from separate perspectives.

Krishna urges Arjuna to perform his duties wholeheartedly while Jesus describes the human eye as the light source for the entire body and the Quran stresses reliability in performing actions. Focus serves to embrace the real world rather than withdrawing from it according to these teachings.

People commonly err by trying to seek concentration as though it exists as a final destination to acquire and retain. The true purpose of concentration serves as a pathway to success rather than representing itself as a final achievement. Mastery functions in the same way as fire does when it serves as the energy that powers cooking. Straining for it results in its instant disappearance. Utilizing concentration as an instrument of transformation will upgrade the quality of all your actions.

A key to growing concentration exists in complete presence in the current moment. Your complete attention should flow towards your work when you are working. If you're listening, truly listen. While engaging in practice make yourself completely focused on the exercise at hand. All leading artists together with athletes and thinkers have practiced this basic truth in their lives. Getting a steady mind happens through complete awareness during the act of showing up which is the simplest way to overcome this challenge.

You should just accept your distracted state without any internal battle when such moments occur. Return your mind back to its present state without_force. Again and again. That's the real practice. Usage of this practice over time leads to diminished mental restlessness. Your actions become more precise. Your professional activities together with personal relationships along with inner tranquility gradually become deeper.

Real concentration possesses the capacity to transform your performance. The practice of concentration leads people to emotional bonding rather than achieving control. True connection with your work leads to a complete transition of everything.

In a moment of reflection about the essence of life have you ever assumed such a position?

We need to understand the forces that guide our progression and resist our advancement along with the factor that separates those with inner direction from the rest who float aimlessly through life. This substantial inquiry needs us to analyze it through a discussion between friends. No heavy stuff, just real talk.

We should explore meditation which involves paying attention to inner self over traditional cave-like meditation methods. Almost no one can manage it easily while multiple settings exist which block its achievement completely. Right after a big meal? Nope. In the middle of a crowd? Forget it. Scrolling through your phone mindlessly? Definitely not. Occasions arise where meditation occurs naturally to you—whoever you are—in the morning before eating and when you are alone and located within a simple room devoid of distractions. Your mind becomes present during those times when it is wide awake. Makes sense, right? Deep thinking requires complete attention since mental focus becomes difficult during distraction periods or when people lose themselves to comfort or constantly seek entertainment.

Now, let's talk about purpose. The real deal. Everyone who reaches tremendous achievements displays an exceptionally clear direction regardless of whether they reach it spiritually or in life. Great historical leaders like Alexander the Great and Buddha as well as Christ and Muhammad did not simply roam aimlessly instead they had clear directions in life. They had purpose. A direction. People needed this purpose to rise each morning despite any obstacles that tried to halt their progress. Such energetic force drives the development of movements which later transform both countries and personal existence.

But purpose isn't just about grand achievements. It's in the small things too. It's the student who pushes through to finish their work. The athlete who keeps training despite the setbacks. The parent who wakes up every day to take care of their family, even when they're exhausted. Purpose isn't about being famous or remembered—it's about knowing why you do what you do and sticking to it.

Fear? That's what holds most people back. Fear of failure, fear of judgment, fear of not being good enough. But here's the thing—fear is just a feeling. It comes and goes. It's like a wave. You either let it drown you, or you learn to ride it. The Bhagavad Gita says, 'You have the right to perform your duty, but never to the fruits of your work.' Meaning? Do what you're meant to do, and let go of the worry about success or failure. The Quran reminds us, 'Indeed, with hardship comes ease.' You struggle, you grow. That's how it's always been.

And let's not forget self-control. The world will throw distractions at you—money, comfort, easy pleasures. But the strongest people? They don't get lost in all that. They know when to step back, when to say no, when to focus on what actually matters. Doesn't mean you can't enjoy life—just means you're in charge of your actions, not the other way around.

So here's the real takeaway: life isn't about avoiding struggle. It's about moving through it with purpose, discipline, and a little bit of faith. Meditation helps you see clearly. Purpose keeps you steady. Fear? It's just another test. And when you accomplish something—whether big or small—that feeling? That joy? It's real. And it's worth it.

You don't have to be a saint or a philosopher to get this. You just have to start paying attention—to yourself, to your actions, to the energy you put into the world. Because at the end of the day, we're all just trying to figure this out. And maybe, just maybe, the key is simpler than we think.

Do you promise yourself you will perform a specific action but the necessity of the promise suddenly evaporates before execution? The initial start turns into endless life interruptions with countless interruptions until you discover your incomplete goal as a forgotten object in your mental background. Happens all the time, right?

Human life works in an infinite pattern of great plans but few results. After our initial motivation to start fades we make our first move but things change with fatigue and doubts in addition to new interesting distractions that lead us to abandon our projects. Fatigue. Doubt. Fear. A new shiny distraction. The project remains unfinished as we suddenly give up. The project stays half-done. The idea never takes off. The dream remains a dream.

What causes us to stop pursuing goals that we have initiated? The reason we find it difficult to achieve completion remains a mystery. We need a plan to stop the pattern of unfinished objectives from recurring.

Let me tell you a story. I took up the project of making a little wooden canoe sometime ago. Not a big deal, just a fun little challenge. First week? Great. Every evening during that time I worked diligently at removing pieces from the wooden block. Second week? My hands hurt from the project while I spent time watching the new movie release. The third week arrived with my attention fully absorbed in movie rewatching while I generated excuses for my lack of work. That canoe? The unfinished canoe stared at me whenever I passed it through the months it spent on the workbench. It took me two complete years to return to complete the unfinished work.

Sounds familiar? The version of your narrative may include something beyond canoes as the core project. You probably delayed your objectives including writing a book or launching a business concept as well as creating a new habit. No one needs to know specific details of your actions since the fundamental design remains all that counts.

People typically hold off until they find absolute perfection to start what they need to accomplish. Too many people believe motivation serves as their main problem. But motivation is fleeting—it's unreliable. Following through requires the establishment of motion instead of waiting for inspiration.

Regular repetition of the technique called "temptation bundling" functioned as a valuable tool according to me. I merged canoe work with my enthusiast activity by turning the task into a musical experience while I worked. The task shifted to an enjoyable present experience instead of a repetitive work-out process. That tiny shift? Game-changer.

Each of us encounters similar challenges like the ones Esther experienced. Esther struggled with endless thinking as she dreamed about opening her baking business in the world while holding her office job. She devoted her days to planning instead of productive work. Once the time was available for her to act she chose to stay preoccupied. Instead of laziness the burden from self-prescribed and outside pressures rendered her incapable of action.

What prevents people from actually accomplishing their objectives? The main blockers of success usually stem from four elements.

The art of concentration means maintaining your target visibility through all distractions. When focus is absent you lose concentration on ten different projects which ensures you finish none.

The practice of self-discipline requires you to appear for tasks that seem unappealing. Building self-discipline entails teaching yourself to execute important actions rather than simpler tasks.

Action represents the fundamental aspect that must happen in order to achieve anything. Planning alongside thinking holds its place but the time comes to execute the task. Perfection in hesitation never measures up to imperfect actual action.

The power to continue moving forward remains strong as the first excitement fades through all obstacles and steady progress slows down. The fundamental aspect of follow-through rests in this element.

These elements work together as different body sections. Focus serves as the head of your performance because it positions your thoughts within the active gameplay. Discipline maintains our position upright just like a healthy backbone. Through action you achieve progress because it provides your hands and feet for movement. And persistence? Through persistence the heart maintains continuous life.

And the best part? The process of mastering focus and discipline does not require immediate simultaneous execution. Just start somewhere. Achieving significant accomplishments results from performing small repeated actions over time. Leave your mentalnees for a new direction because action supersedes hesitation to finish tasks.

Reality dictates nobody will provide the perfect opportunity without our own determination. The process of creation starts with daily attendance so pervious obstacles shift into daily habits.

So, what's your canoe? What matters most is when precisely you will complete it.

The process of dreaming big generally appears as a simple effortless experience to all of us. I mean, really big. People envision themselves making consistent workouts early in the day while constructing their best business venture coupled with literary success and meaningful impact. Our vision remains fresh at this moment so winning already appears to be on the horizon. Reality appears to disrupt these fantasies bringing along the task of actual follow-through. That's a whole different story.

We should avoid self-criticism after failing to achieve what we began because there are unique circumstances to consider. Why is it so hard? A society based solely on talent and intelligence would result in universal completion of goals. But it's not. The real issue stems from something profound which causes cognitive confusion even ahead of our initial genuine action.

## The Illusion of Movement

We love to plan. Human minds enjoy developing mental plans more than they enjoy executing them. The dopamine release activates when we start something because it feels like we achieve progress in our lives. But planning isn't doing. The internal process of planning mountain ascent differs vastly from the actual physical action of boot-wearing for climbing.

When you foresee every aspect of your upcoming project you tend to achieve the feeling of completion before you begin. Our brains use this deception to fool human mind. Productive procrastination pushes individuals to stay endlessly in between starting tasks and reaching targets.

## The Resistance Within

Most people construct abstract barriers which restrain their growth.

Trying something risks that it may fail even though attempting leads to failure. What if I look foolish? What if I waste my time? Instead of exposing ourselves to potential failure we decide that waiting holds greater value.

The perfectionist part of ourselves states we must first wait for the perfect opportunity or work on additional preparation. Perfectionism represents nothing more than fear which dons a sophisticated disguise.

The way the modern world functions specifically targets what matters most through distraction methods. Ouranos and Lycaon provide six of the unique names found within Hesiod's poem Theogony. Hesiod authored Theogony in the 8th century before the common era. As we continue to carry out this method we turn into soldiers who stop fighting for their real desires because they become exhausted from carrying their weapons.

Willingness to control oneself without proper discipline proves unfaithful. Discipline functions as a method that works alongside habitual processes before turning into your established pattern. Our failure to establish this foundation forces us to wait for motivation to rescue us because as we all know genuine motivation avoids us most of the time.

After unsuccessful completion we should refrain from self-blame because different conditions apply to each situation. Why is it so hard? When a society depends only on mental aptitude and intellectual skill every goal would achieve 100% success rate. But it's not. The fundamental problem derives from an underlying factor that leads to confusion in thinking before people start genuine action.

Has it happened to you that you feel entrapped in a continuous cycle? You continuously move forward with action but somehow remain stationary while deep down you understand there is no actual movement. Humans rarely recognize the occurrence of this phenomenon. A cycle of busyness consumes our minds although it does not exist in reality. We constantly maintain that we have already pushed ourselves to the limit. Would we recognize reality when we eliminated everything we have right now? Have you ever considered observing your life while being completely transparent to your own self? The reality would emerge if we examined our actions with honesty that we consistently evade significant things.

It's funny, isn't it? At the beginning we bring enormous enthusiasm and high energy into new ventures. But then? We stall. We get distracted. We make excuses. Our minds create various explanations regarding the failed relationships. And the easiest thing to do? Stay where we are. It's comfortable. It's convenient. We perhaps conceal a small degree of nervousness deep inside. Scared of what's out there. We fear negative consequences when we decide to execute our intentions.

We should examine a hypothetical situation where we actually executed the plan? We should move beyond dreams that remain in our thoughts by transforming them into concrete realities. Following through everything should become our daily practice.

Yeah, it's the harder path. This commitment holds the most importance. Your life takes a new direction when you choose to finish all the work you initiate. You stop wasting time. The shift occurs from living in future expectations to beginning progress toward genuine ambitions. Your goals? They stop being just ideas. Achieving these goals becomes reachable targets.

And it's not just about work. A trustworthy person sets themselves up for success by believing in both themselves and their close relationships. Being someone who finishes their assignments establishes you as a person others recognize. Your word carries weight. All those who matter in your life you have taught to depend on your follow-through commitments because they trust your performance. You establish self-belief because trusting yourself becomes your reality. You stop second-guessing. Living with clarity sets in since you understand your ability to complete whatever challenge life brings.

Real life demands that we understand the truth behind this reality. We hit walls. We lose motivation. That fire we started with? It flickers. Lack of understanding about the reasons behind these failures leads to continuous repetition of similar mistakes.

Think about it—what stops us? A mix of things. Some practical, some psychological. The main impediments to goal achievement come from pursuing unrealistic targets and procrastinating along with choosing inappropriate objectives. Quick dopamine dosages pull us toward distractions making us abandon the actual work in the process. Our ability to reach our ambitions is held up by multiple factors that include apprehension about failure combined with concerns about judgment and perfectionism and poor self-knowledge of our personal aspirations.

Now, take a step back. Look at your life. Do you execute the goals you stated you wanted to achieve? Your life remains fixated in persistent recurring habits.

Worry not because many people experience this situation. The good news? There's a way forward. The process begins when we fully recognize our real obstacles followed by proactive change.

## *Staying Hungry*

Let's talk about motivation. Which true forces motivate you to execute your actions? At what point during the persistent work phase do you maintain your drive?

The dream she had involved creating a charity organization to assist people in need. It was her passion. But the reality? Harder than she expected. The fundraising together with organizing logistics and battling unlimited challenges completely exhausted her. She turned off her passion entirely in a short period of time. She quit. Those who observed her questioned why a person would drop something important to them.

The problem? None of her plan accounted for experiencing difficulty. She directed all her attention toward her dream without paying attention to the steps needed to turn it into reality. She burned out due to lacking a profound foundation of motivation.

Passion exists as an insufficient force for achieving success. You need something stronger. A true source of motivation. A force which maintains your stability when life presents tough situations.

So what fuels motivation? Your motivation arises from balancing three fundamental elements.

Your goal contains meanings that matter deeply to yourself.

The rewards recognized through completion emerge as the advantages you acquire after finishing.

The lack of performing this task results in significant problems that one faces.

Our drive normally decreases when we disconnect from one of these essential factors.

Humans possess two types of motivation which are labeled external and internal motivation.

## *External Motivation*

External forces generate external motivation through combinations of fear of failure and pressure from others or mandatory accountability partners. External motivation demonstrates its strength because everyone wants to maintain a good standing with others. The need to answer to another person creates strong motivational force.

But the real magic? Internal motivation.

## Internal Motivation

Fire that begins inside yourself represents internal motivation. Understanding drives you because of your life mission instead of pushing you through the power of fear. Your work becomes unblockable when it represents what you truly are combined with finding meaning in your daily tasks.

In order to find clarity consider what matters most to you right now. What do you truly care about? During difficult times what force will empower you to advance?

Following through exceeds traditional ideas about self-discipline in life. It's about knowing yourself. Knowledge about your fears together with your distractions alongside your genuine motivations will help you progress forward.

Have you taken sufficient preparation to execute the tasks?

Many individuals start with setting goals along with establishing plans while experiencing initial enthusiasm yet later experience cessation. It happens to everyone. The normal flow of life together with distracting elements causes the moment when you lose grip of important goals that matter to you.

So, how do we stay on track? We require strategies to continue moving ahead during moments of waning motivation. To succeed in life one needs strategic planning more than sheer willpower.

## The Power of Accountability

Making an uphill cart push alone becomes an impossible task. It's tough. Having a support group working with you represents a powerful scenario. Accountability groups function as this type of assistance. The commitment strength rises when different people have entrusted you with their words since they expect you to follow through. Your commitment becomes stronger because you do not want to disappoint your support network. Each member in the group supports one another so the primary player stays on track when someone else steps away from the group. Wise management of shame creates it into a powerful tool for motivation.

## The Money Factor: A Little Skin in the Game

People often treat their purchased items more valuably after making financial payments. The payment of monetary dues for gym memberships and online courses creates valuable loss from stopping participation that makes the decision of quitting feel financially wasteful. The same motivational process also applies to goal achievement.

A proof of commitment requires financial stakes through which you ensure your follow-through. Put money on the line. Engage a life coach while enrolling in training sessions with your funds secured by a trusted person until you achieve your targets. A financial commitment takes the place of your simple promise.

## Bribing Yourself (Yes, It Works)

Every one of us finds great motivation in receiving rewards as a form of appreciation. So, use that. You should create an incentive for reaching your individual performance targets. You can achieve these personal goals through trips or fancy dinners or entirely guiltless days of idleness. To earn the reward you must feel it was properly deserved. Your knowledge of the fabulous destination at the goal becomes something that simplifies your path.

**The Motivating Factors That Govern Human Transformation Consist of Fear and Desire**

People shift residences because they want to escape negative elements such as failure atrocities and regrets yet others migrate for their desired accomplishments. People choose to move after locating success or building dreams together with achieving their version of a perfect life.

Which one drives you more? If fear works, use it. When desire functions as your driving force you should concentrate your energy in that direction. Either way, know your why. Are your true reasons behind this decision clear to you? How does it change your life? The movement impacts receiving love from people in your inner circle.

## The Cost of Doing Nothing

Every choice has a cost. Pursuing your goal means giving up certain aspects of time and effort as well as potential comfort concessions. Not pursuing your goals results in what loss? What do you lose? Growth? Opportunities? A better life? Discovering what we will lose whenever we remain stationary proves to be the best motivation to advance.

## Keep It in Front of You

Motivation becomes weak because we fail to maintain awareness of our reasons for motivation. You must place motivational visual reminders nearby which could include pictures notes or special objects that keep your objective in sight. Shift your stimuli around each few days because your brain will lose its capacity to retain focus.

## The Big Takeaway

Seek individuals who will maintain responsibility for your progress. Alone, it's easy to quit.

Financial investment works as a motivation tool since no one likes losing their money.

Bribe yourself. Rewards work.

Find your why. Fear or desire—what moves you?

When you do nothing your effort remains countless.

Keep motivation in sight—literally.

# VIII

# Establish only three main goals per day

Discipline requires strength only during select periods in daily life. Building a system which makes continuation easier than stopping completely is what truly matters. So, what's your system?

Every person understands the experience of maintaining endless tasks in their daily planning. Your intention starts with writing ten activities but you only complete zero tasks out of those ten items. Overwhelm kicks in. To stay afloat in your work prioritize three important tasks per day. That's it.

Better outcomes result from this strategy rather than reduced workload. Prioritizing. According to the Quran you should accomplish mīzān through balancing your efforts. Absorbing yourself in every task results in a failure to complete any work. Giving complete focus to three selected tasks allows you to experience inevitable success.

## *Set Boundaries and Non-Negotiables*

Freedom emerges as the natural outcome of disciplinary practice instead of experiencing restriction. Tapas represents self-discipline according to the Vedas which helps people reach their higher objectives. Creating specific rules for yourself will transform your life into something better because of their clarity.

Begin this exercise by creating two lists of five things which must be accomplished every day and five things you refuse to permit.

## *Example:*

Strict requirements include thirty minutes of daily writing alongside exercise before you invest time into new knowledge and practice wholesome eating and nightly reflection.

I reject the behaviors of social media automation, selective exercise care, acceptance of interruptions and procrastinating vital responsibilities with self-harm actions.

Guardrails help you minimize your mental exhaustion which results from making too many choices. Your guidelines function independently to perform the tasks.

## *Your Manifesto: Your Personal Guidebook*

The manifesto functions as an agreement that you create for yourself. Your direction takes precedence over attaining the state of being perfect. The manifesto keeps reminding you during tough times and moments when you want to surrender to show what you basically represent.

Jesus mentions in the Bible that individuals must construct their houses upon rock foundations instead of unstable sand bases. A strong foundation withstands the storms. The foundation of your manifesto will keep you upright during moments when motivation disappears.

Seize today to write down your very own manifesto. Keep it simple, keep it real. And most importantly, follow it.

## *People who persist each day become the winners.*

Let's talk about something real. At some point everyone finds themselves at an important decision point with a path to growth and a path to comfort as their options. We've all been there. According to the Bhagavad Gita our inner struggle occurs when our elevate soul tries to fight against the aspect that desires comfort. Numerous scriptures including the Bible, the Quran as well as the Vedas present the basic truth about how discipline controls one's life direction.

The main issue arises because we tend to relate discipline with pure force of will but willpower often proves unstable. Some days, you feel unstoppable. Some days rising from sleep requires a fierce fight against oneself. That's where rules come in. Establish goals that match who you wish to become rather than following rules from society because they help you stay on track with your identity.

Your energy requires protective boundaries that should be established as your first rule.

The essence of discipline does not require you to work your body until it breaks. Self-discipline means you should identify how various activities affect your energy levels both positively and negatively.

You announce that social media limit will remain at 30 minutes daily yet you browse. Your attention deserves sacred protection which is the true reason for establishing boundaries even when social media itself is not an evil. The choice is set to read for twenty minutes each day to satisfy your intellectual hunger. Setting boundaries lets vital aspects enter your life without overwhelming your self while protecting your valued energy.

**As Arjuna stood** helpless on the battlefield Krishna did not advise him to depend on temporary motivation. The sage showed him understanding of his true life mission. The personal code of conduct which defines you belongs to your personal dharma. Your set boundaries keep showing you your life purpose because emotions sometimes want to divert you from your path.

Let's talk about something real. People sometimes need to make important life decisions that require them to choose whether progress is more important than comfort. We've all been there. According to the Bhagavad Gita our inner struggle occurs when our elevate soul tries to fight against the aspect that desires comfort. Numerous scriptures including the Bible, the Quran as well as the Vedas present the basic truth about how discipline controls one's life direction.

## The fifth rule teaches us to maintain our word to our own self

You never retreat from commitments which you made to friends so why do it to yourself? Keeping promises to yourself holds the same value as any other promise which means you should never break them.

The act of hitting snooze after promising to wake up early conflicts with your subconscious belief regarding your spoken words. Your self-respect strengthens whenever you honor your own promises regardless of their size. Self-respect operates as the single driving force that produces discipline more than any other thing.

## *You Are the Architect of Your Life*

The rules exist to deliver true freedom to everyone. You gain sovereignty against mistimed discouragement as well as erratic tendencies alongside continuous beginning and ending behavior.

Select several rules which become your personal choice while monitoring your life begin to transform. Discipline should never be a form of self-harm because it enables you to create a life you will genuinely enjoy living.

**Human beings** continuously pursue targets throughout their existence. A goal represents one thing whereas a habit stands as another alongside the desired version of our self which we perceive for ourselves. Each day we battle against various interruptions alongside personal urges that whisper to us "Postpone it." There exists a basic method which can help you escape this pattern.

Putting off an unproductive decision can be achieved by waiting for ten minutes next time you feel the urge. That's it. Just ten. The choice is yours to proceed if you desire the outcome afterward. Simple momentary delays create an opportunity for us to eliminate impulsive behavior while establishing disciplined behavior patterns.

You can also leverage this method to fight off feelings of quitting good tasks because "Ten more minutes" serves as your reminder. Continue persisting for an additional brief period rather than giving up completely. That little delay, that small push, compounds into something bigger over time. You build your ability to exert self-control by subdividing significant changes into little by little achievable stages.

Workers construct discipline via persistent decisions made throughout regular daily activities instead of relying on dramatic massive changes. Your mind becomes stronger each time you practice waiting and every time you continue for an additional ten minutes. Through this you regain authority over yourself after having lost control to your impulsive behavior.

Now, let's talk about rules. Most people don't like rules. Rules help us maintain simplicity in life though people may or may not acknowledge the fact. These rules eliminate all sources of uncertainty while clearing out mental doubt and hesitancy. The Bhagavad Gita together with the Bible and Quran and Vedas provide direction to humanity through structured guidelines rather than options overload. The system functions to free people from the freeze caused by continuous decision-making.

## *Here are a few simple ones:*

You base your actions on laziness? You should question this answer. Do you want to keep this behavior if you are trying to build a likeness of yourself?

Three major tasks a day—maximum. You must differentiate between tasks that matter the most and those that must be handled right away from distracting unimportant work.

Create daily limitations and requirements. Building consistency leads to the development of real power according to the author.

Establish your intentions about what you need to do while defining clear boundaries of what you will perform as well as the activities you refuse to handle. Clarity cuts through self-doubt.

You should examine how you will evolve during future time spans starting from ten minutes to ten days and ten hours to yourself. Stand proud when you think about your current decision choice.

It's just ten minutes. Ten minutes represents the minimal time needed for you to keep resisting temptations or survive uncomfortable situations.

All other factors become irrelevant when you lack the proper mental approach. Following through is entirely mental. Direction of your thoughts requires mental training to view matters differently.

## *Mindset 1: It's Worth It*

Believing effort counts as hard work outweighs physical strain because it contains the most difficulty. Your commitment to the learning process enhances your motivation which reduces your chances of surrendering while doing it. A student who faces academic challenges in their studies can help explain this mindset. People who achieve success lack supreme intelligence yet maintain the conviction that their efforts will produce positive results. And that applies to life too.

## *Mindset 2: Get Comfortable with Discomfort*

No one likes feeling uncomfortable. The process of meaningful transformation together with sustainable expansion exists solely beyond personal comfort boundaries. The Gita describes detachment as a state which separates people from short-lived pleasures rather than their very existence. Sitting in uncomfortable situations without escape reveals our hidden power of resistance against adversities.

## Mindset 3: Learn from Everything

Whatever you do in life becomes a lesson for yourself. Your path leads either to success or towards gaining knowledge about wrong approaches that require modification. But quitting? That teaches you nothing. The perception that all situations carry lessons enables you to lose your fear of failure.

Mindset 4: Take control of stress before it controls you

A majority of our failures stem from sources other than lack of capability. Our failure occurs when stress along with overwhelming situations or unfavorable mental states take over. An exhausted mind leads to the destruction of your willpower. The care you give your mental and physical well-being remains essential over any other consideration thus self-care through meditation rest exercise and deep breathing should not be considered a premium. It's a necessity.

## Chapter 5: The Art of Beating Procrastination

So, let's talk about it—procrastination. You know what it feels like. Even though you have huge work to complete you make the decision to pursue all the other tasks instead. Between phone scrolling and desk cleaning there emerges an urge to reply to a message sent three weeks earlier. Time passes swiftly until your deadline becomes urgent forcing you into complete panic.

But why do we do this? What makes each of us intentionally destroy the opportunities we have to succeed?

## The Two Versions of You

You have two versions of yourself who exist together in the moment—the Present You and the Future You. Future You is ambitious. Future You sets goals. Future You has sworn to start his morning by exercising at the gym following a 5 AM wake-up before finishing his work before noon.

Future You as an entity does not exist in reality because time only recognizes Present You as the existing reality. Only Present You does. And Present You? Present You only desires to spend the current time happily. Your current self considers this approach an excellent concept. One more show must play before starting according to Present You.

This is called time inconsistency. Your brain gives much higher value to instant pleasures compared to future benefits. Your dreams appear perfect in theory but turn out challenging to accomplish in real life because of this effect.

## The Trick: Make the Future Feel Like the Present

Work with our brain wiring since changes are impossible because we must operate with the given cognitive functions instead of fighting against them. Temptation bundling serves as the key solution during this process.

Choosing temptation bundling is similar to establishing personal promises between multiple activities. You combine the unappealing task that needs completion with something satisfying that you truly desire. Your habit of listening to music pairs perfectly with the unappealing chore work. You promise yourself that listening to your preferred songs is the only thing that will make dish-washing tolerable. Your thinking links the uninteresting work with pleasant experiences.

## Here are some examples:

Only watch Netflix while exercising.

You must consume your optimal caffeine fix when completing that challenging task.

Playing podcasts should be restricted to your ride between office and home.

Your present self cooperates with your future self by following this technique. And guess what? It works.

Start Small: The Pebble Approach

People tend to procrastinate because a given task appears overwhelming rather than being forced to delay it out of laziness. The approach to solving problems lies in dividing large tasks into minuscule components. The approach is similar to building a staircase on a large structure. The correct approach to handling overwhelming obstacles is by beginning with the placement of tiny stones over the barrier. Building stones into a step-by-step process will eventually lead you to success.

If writing a report stands as your requirement then begin by focusing on just one single paragraph for now. Begin your task by committing to writing only one paragraph instead of stating your goal of generating twenty pages. A single paragraph appears to be an easy goal to accomplish. When you begin working on a task typically you will discover enough energy to continue moving ahead.

## Fear Can Be a Powerful Ally

The unexpected revelation states that fear itself proves useful against procrastination. Not in a paralyzing way, but in a motivating way.

People engage in overnight study sessions before exams due to experiencing fear about their performance. Because fear kicks in. The stakes become real. Your mind suddenly grasps the impending danger of starting late to become failed.

Successful individuals rely on productive paranoia as their regular approach to daily tasks. Bill Gates maintained a constant state of worrying about potential failure which made him stay vigilant while remaining actively responsive. People who struggle with procrastination should answer these questions to themselves:

Will anything bad occur if I fail to execute this task within schedule?

What's the worst-case scenario?

Could I lose an opportunity?

One small feeling of fear can possibly drive you to initiate necessary tasks.

Your current self displays no concern for what will happen to your future self. Here and now rewards are what it wants rather than postponing gratification. Procrastination works better when you reset your mind to feel things as they happen now.

**Temptation bundling works.** The combination of one enjoyable activity alongside another unpleasant one will cause your negative experience to lose its power over you.

Start ridiculously small. Your small initial step creates more steps which automatically turn into motion towards your goal.

Maintain fear at proper levels since it delivers benefits while excessive fear leads to negative consequences. While short periods of pressure stay focused it becomes counterproductive to maintain extreme nervousness.

The struggle to defeat procrastination never requires flawlessness from you. In order to be effective at this technique you must learn how your mind functions. Set systems which provide better incentives for action than doing nothing because you ought to begin before seeking motivational sparks.

Guests in grocery stores experience specific arrangements that lure them into purchasing unwanted food items. You enter the store with positive goals in mind to buy fresh fruits and whole grain products without getting extravagant. The checkout area features candy bars together with chips and soda which are temptingly positioned near shoppers at the last moment. Your mental focus turns dull while standing at checkout since you feel drained and wish to leave. You suddenly grasp a chocolate bar without realizing how it happened since you lacked decision-making power.

This isn't an accident. Humans are constantly drawn by external forces that move them away from their authentic desires. The Bhagavad Gita reflects upon the unstable human mind which shifts eagerly between multiple topics just like Arjuna experienced on the battlefield. We find ourselves battling daily against the forces of distractions and impulses that fail to benefit our lives.

So what do we do? People need to design their environment to determine its influence over them.

Working at a disorganized workplace requires you to create order. The best approach to stop repetitive phone scrolling is to move the device to a different room. A distracted mind that experiences no temptations becomes capable of making deliberate decisions.

The research at Cornell University demonstrates this fact. People consumed two times more candy when placed in clear containers on their desks but only ate half as much when the candies were hidden in opaque containers separated by a few feet away. Current research shows that physical removal prevents mental awareness of things hence providing you with action control.

We need to view this principle regarding candy but extend its application to additional categories as well. The things that distract you from discipline element are possibly mental not only physical entities but equally habits and social interactions too. The sacred texts of the Quran mention disruptive thoughts which separate believers from their spiritual path while Jesus frequently left quiet spaces to engage in prayer according to the Bible. Why? Because the environment matters.

Your environment determines your ability to hear external noise so much that your focus turns to noise itself. The arrangement you make for discipline will automatically establish your disciplined lifestyle.The entire decision-making process is included within this phenomenon. Studies show that countries which enroll people automatically as donors achieve a 95% participation rate but countries that require consent only get 27% donorship. Barely 27%. People prefer to avoid decision-making hence they choose the default option.

Now, apply that to your life. What's your default setting? Where do you keep your food supply: cookies located on the counter or do you prefer having fruit at a similar spot? Your phone stands on your desk or across the distance of the room. Getting to your running shoes requires ease of access because they rest either on top or hidden beneath other items in your space. Everyone possesses enough strength to maintain their resolve; making appropriate decisions should remain the most convenient options.

And let's talk about attention. All of us experience moments when we feel unable to concentrate. Your brain lacks the ability to perform quick task-switching because it functioned differently for its design. Sophie Leroy discovered within a study that people lose parts of their attention on former tasks after fast task switches. Open computer windows that you do not observe cause everything to operate steadily slower.

People who engage in multitasking activities actually fall into an intellectual trap rather than displaying any skill. Those who perform multiple moving tasks simultaneously display declining ability to block disruptions. Science, psychology and both traditional wisdom systems such as the Gita and Vedas and contemporary analysis agree that absolute concentration flows only from a unified state of mind. Through yoga training a person acquires the ability to observe equivalence throughout all things according to Krishna. That's clarity. That's presence.

Your true existence depends on whether you choose design as your life path or allow events to determine your path. By doing only a couple of straightforward adjustments such as removing distraction points and establishing better default settings and staying focused on tasks you will surpass many others.

According to the spiritual teachings that science later verified: The essence of your being has no relation to your errant thoughts or impulsive actions or fleeting distractions. The essence of your being comes from your regularly selected choices. The best method for making successful choices involves simplifying the process.

## *At this moment which change can you implement?*

People seem to be preoccupied with working multiple tasks at the same time like they will reach greater productivity while actually making themselves exhausted. Most of us function like circus performers through multitasking only to exhaust ourselves without any real progress. Many people now seek social status through public displays of busy-ness while embracing multitasking as their honorary symbol. The effectiveness of simultaneous accomplishment remains doubtful when considering reality.

Humans were not born with endless multitasking capacities in their minds. Wisdom in the ancient Bhagavad Gita identifies 'Ekagrata' as the force of total concentration. The Bible identifies that serving two masters remains impossible. According to the Quran true effectiveness stems from pure and honest purposes. The Vedas describe deep focused mental state as 'Dhyana'. Every religious teaching proves that Landmark your attention leads to actual growth and mastery.

Science backs this up, too. Scientific research confirms that excessive multitasking leads to overall performance decline in all aspects. Multiple leaky cups cannot efficiently receive a water pour which results in all cups remaining empty. When the mind faces excessive information it leads to increased interruptions which gradually extend work time from thirty minutes to many hours. You experience a common situation when you move between different apps to check your email while scrolling and responding to messages during crucial work periods. Each day finishes before you recognize how the hours escaped without your awareness.

So what's the alternative? Single tasking. Despite seeming easy this methodology becomes a breakthrough due to modern technology that distracts people at every turn. Devoting yourself to single activities means complete and absolute attention to the task. When you work, just work. When you eat, just eat. Although talking with someone requires active attention. The essence of singletasking emerges from being fully present while silencing abstract thinking.

Distractions will continue to persist even though they will not vanish right away. The key is awareness. Start noticing when you drift. Practice bringing your attention consistently back to the present work requirement. Maintain a ready notepad near you to record distracting thoughts which will appear rather than rush to action at the moment. The objective is not to be inflexible yet it forces us toward purposeful action.

The practice of batching allows you to gather similar tasks because it reduces the mental burden of constant equipment switching. Henry Ford originated manufacturing assembly lines which advise how think about this process. Tedious daily work becomes more efficient when you commit blocks of time to handle one activity at a time. Email response sessions should be scheduled times instead of constant five-minute checks. Make every phone call during a specific period. Your brain will use your decision to appreciate it.

Another game-changer? The 'Don't-Do' list. Most of us are familiar with to-do lists but have we considered creating a list of activities which we should prevent ourselves from doing? One of the many activities which starts your day negatively is scrolling through social media upon waking up. Saying the affirmative response at every opportunity. The perfecting of something beyond what it needs goes against productivity. When you eliminate activities which exhaust you then essential responsibilities and meaningful activities will find their space.

Clarity emerges as the fundamental goal once the day concludes. Your true objective regarding the direction of your time along with your daily efforts should become clear. The essence of life consists of pursuing meaningful activities which create peace within you rather than filling every minute with additional tasks. The power of the mind becomes its most brilliant when it concentrates its radiance on a single direction. Spending some time at ease during today will help you accomplish this goal. Devote your attention to only what you do at a specific moment. The true magic often presents itself after focusing on meaningful activities.

There are times when multiple responsibilities pull you away from your current tasks. Time pulls you in multiple directions while something else demands your time always. Feels exhausting, right? Understanding which activities to avoid represents the actual key instead of focusing solely on accomplishing more tasks.

Think about it. People create to-do lists throughout each day. These systems are supposed to help both productivity and life organization. The essential element for changing our performance lies not within items on our to-do lists rather within intentional omissions. Keeping track of what we should not do became a practice.

During the Bhagavad Gita on the battlefield Arjuna should have ignored all pointless deliberation about each possible option to make a decision. The spiritual advice Krishna gives states that Arjuna must act now through insightful action rather than seek endless analysis. The same idea applies to us. Using energy on insignificant matters will exhaust our capacity for targeting important tasks.

Absolute perfection should remain avoided because it acts as a deceptive trap. Most people seek absolute certainty before deciding but finding the perfect moment often leads them to miss the opportunity entirely. According to his principle Colin Powell said that entering a decision requires you to have at least 40% of the information available while keeping it under 70%. Not before. Not after. Without 40% or more of necessary information your choice lacks any rational basis. More than 70%, you're overthinking.

This understanding exists universally because it appears in all spiritual teachings including Gita and Vedas and also in the Bible and Quran. Lack of action because of excessive planning results in psychological stagnation. Prophet Muhammad outlined taking action through steady progression instead of standing by for a magnificent opportunity to materialize perfectly.

When facing a writing challenge you should think about whether you require additional research information or merely require some mind-free time.

Moving on to a different topic we should investigate the monumental power inherent in inactivity. Yeah, you heard me. Doing nothing. Not scrolling. Not reading. Just being. The human mind generates its most profound insights when it exists in a state of complete relaxation. Retrospectively termed meditation or mindfulness yet practical to anyone through simple ceiling observation works as a technique. Stepping away from something acts as the only effective method to start progressing.

For maintaining a powerful fire you need to allow breaks between wood additions instead of continuous log placement. To achieve this state give it unobstructed space while allowing fresh air and dedicating enough time. Your mind works the same way.

Cut out the unnecessary. The inclusion of items to never perform could be as vital as creating a list of tasks to accomplish.

Maintaining a constant pursuit of flawlessness indicates a single error. The perfect percentage range lies between 40-70%. Keep moving when your current situation lies between 40% and 70%.

Let yourself rest. Real productivity stems from the ability to recognize both movement moments and breathing intervals.

Three things in order successfully executed result in experiencing lighter life and less overwhelming work while accomplishing more in your daily activities. Your movement achieves clarity which leads to more accomplishment rather than exceeding effort.

**And that? That's the real power move.**

# IX

# Failure patterns persist with solutions

Life often puts you in repetitive patterns without any sign of relief. You attempt with everything you have but outcomes appear different from what you originally pictured.

Michael felt that way. He began running his business from dreams which he thought would transform his life suddenly. It didn't. His former love of his work disappeared as he felt exhausted while doing nothing but postpone tasks and dislike what had been his labor of passion. The task of insisting upon improper routines and excessive caffeine intake to battle his natural night preference gave him no desired outcomes.

At that moment he realized discipline along with effort might not be the real problem. The disruptive expectations he had might have caused his problems.

## *The Trap of False Hope*

Transformation appeals to most of us. Transitioning into a new mindset together with new behaviors and a fresh life brings about complete changes. But change is rarely instant. According to the Bhagavad Gita "One's own self stands as both ally and adversary in the path of life." Nobody ever wins or loses battles rather than themselves.

The deceptive inner voice repeatedly states that this time everything will improve for the better. People struggle to achieve transformation because they attempt too much at once. People expect to transform into someone with unmatched self-control upon rising tomorrow. Disappointment becomes a powerful force which strikes immediately after such unsuccessful attempts.

The process of actual change advances through scheduled phases rather than single jumps. Making only modest and consistent improvements leads to the changes that become permanent. You will set yourself up for failure if you try to change everything all at once so establish what small steps you can take for today. Michael succeeded in creating his routine through method adaptation rather than insisting to fit into a system which did not match his nature.

## The Overthinking Spiral

It might appear to be advancement yet it really is not. Overthinking.

The research has begun and every potential scenario is under thorough examination. It's productive, right? Nope. Activity in most cases exists exclusively as a false perception.

The Quran emphasizes trust and effort because sometimes you need to move forward without knowing every single detail as stated in "Indeed, with hardship, there is ease." (94:6)

Everyone has experienced researching basic choices like mobile phone selection yet emerged in higher confusion than their starting point. That's the paradox of choice. Throughout the option selection process the act of deciding grows exponentially more difficult.

The trick? Limit your options. Focus on what actually matters. Make a decision, and move on.

## Worrying: The Mind's Useless Gym Workout

People believe worrying brings them important preparation although it serves no useful purpose. Energy depletion occurs as a result of the situation while it seems unproductive.

Jesus declared through Matthew 6:27 that worrying cannot increase the length of life even by one hour. Exactly.

We suffer two times whenever we worry since we endure psychological stress in addition to possibly facing the problematic scenario. Stressing about potential issues ends up producing no result since those problems mostly did not materialize. Prepare yourself by focusing on present action instead of wasting time on future scenarios. At this moment which action should you take to generate substantial outcomes?

Know Yourself, Work With Yourself

Not being aware of your true self will lead you toward continual failures.

According to the Vedas a person can raise their status through mental self-reliance without using self-demeaning methods (Bhagavad Gita 6.5). According to this formula your main enemy should always be your own self as any other adversary would be counterproductive.

The challenge facing Michael stemmed from his attempt to fit into something that was distinctly different from his nature. The complete clarity about his personal energy and patterns and natural rhythms made everything simpler to handle. He accepted his own being by using his natural framework.

Ask yourself:

At what times do I typically possess optimal energy? Work during that time.

I require either serene isolation or ambient sounds. Adjust your environment.

Working with others or functioning without them makes me more productive in my task completion. Find what fits.

The principles that make you strong also serve as efficient tools that you should employ.

Failure isn't the problem. Being unaware of the reasons behind our failures acts as the main issue.

The same patterns show no signs of changing so try new approaches instead of putting in excessive effort. Reduce your goals to reasonable levels as you limit your anxiety through better thinking therefore work with natural strengths instead of fighting against them.

Success isn't about being superhuman. Understanding your own human nature while learning effective approaches to work with your present self stands as success.

## Daily Systems for Success

A meaningful discussion follows today. We all want success. People establish objectives then create strategic plans before executing their goals with great determination. Achieving our goals becomes difficult even when we are extremely motivated yet we do not succeed sometimes. Why is that?

Let me tell you about Ned. Ned established his personal consulting company. The beginning of his business filled him with excitement and passion to seize world opportunities. Everything operated without trouble during the first stage of early rising time followed by email correspondence networking and project achievement. His expanding business created rising responsibilities for him. His inbox exploded. Deadlines piled up. Clients were getting impatient. He was drowning.

Until professionalism and organization collapsed as his workplace became a chaotic field of abandoned papers and mail messages. The stress produced visible signs such as dark circles beneath his eyes and he drank many cups of coffee and ate only fast food throughout each day. Curiously enough the business began showing significant signs of decline when poor ratings started appearing alongside the decline of his client base and fast depletion of his finances.

So, what went wrong? Ned relied only on willpower. The truth about willpower reveals that it operates as fuel for a motor vehicle. It runs out. Your current situation becomes immobilizing after your willpower runs out. A system should replace his current approach of increasing his motivation and working longer hours.

## *A System Will Serve You Better Than Simply Having Motivation*

See, motivation is great. It gets you started. But systems keep you going. Sunrise always occurs regardless of whether the sun remembers its task. Streams of water do not arbitrarily halt their movement. No. Nature runs on systems. And so should we.

Success happens automatically when you establish a system of arranged routines and habits. The system functions as a mechanism that eliminates daily decisions thus saving you mental energy to follow its instructions.

## *Let's break it down.*

## *1. Keep a Scoreboard*

Observation shows that we achieve better results when we monitor our performance. Sports become competitive because the scoreboard provides immediate feedback regarding player performance. By failing to keep track of personal progress people cannot determine whether they succeed or not.

You need to monitor key aspects which matter to you. Maintain continuous scorekeeping for your primary goals regardless of your field or type of accomplishment. Celebration of minor achievements stands as the deciding factor. Scored a new client?

Great success requires a delightful cup of coffee. Finished that project? Taking a walk under such circumstances can make you feel proud. Your success level increases each time you celebrate which allows you to maintain your position in life.

## 2. Master Time, Don't Chase It

All human beings possess an equal share of time no matter where they are situated. Which factors separate successful individuals from the ones who remain unsuccessful? Time management.

Set a routine. The system serves as an organized structure rather than an ordinary list. Decide in advance the hours you devote to work and rest as well as time reserved for activities that maintain your mental state. And most importantly—stick to it.

One powerful trick? Block time for similar tasks. Check emails only during designated sessions instead of continuously. Devote strict time periods to work tasks that eliminate all possible interruptions. Your energy preservation increases when you decrease the number of task shifts you perform.

## 3. Your investment into good habits should be lower than your investment into bad ones

The economics concept of transaction costs refers to hidden business expenses that create obstacles during commercial transactions. Life requires every action to come at a specific expense.

Workspace disorganization causes you to spend 10 minutes to locate one single document. That's a high transaction cost. The single act of organizing your area creates permanent cost reduction benefits. Success elements must become effortless while obstacles which hinder you must remain difficult to overcome.

Want to work out? Keep your gym clothes ready. Complete avoidance of social media scrolling becomes achievable through implementing minor changes.

Make it harder to access. The human brain prefers to follow the path of minimal effort. You should design your good habits for easy completion while you should design your bad habits to become unpleasant.

## 4. Gather Everything Before You Start

Momentum is everything. When you reach the flow state it is interrupted by searches for necessary items. That kills flow. You should collect every requirement including materials and information before beginning any new project. People avoid beginning their onion cutting until they organize all essential cooking components in the kitchen. Life works the same way.

## The Big Picture

Every sacred text combines the Bhagavad Gita with Bible and Quran and Vedas teaches lessons about discipline which require practicing consistently. A person's actions guided by wisdom prove superior to relentless yet confused attempts according to Krishna's teaching to Arjuna.

According to the Bible faith activates through active works since it remains lifeless when work remains inactive. The Quran talks about perseverance. And the Vedas? Everything that comes out of their teachings reveals a focus on rhythmic organization.

Success does not result only from working hard. Professional achievement involves making well-planned systems which lighten your workload.

Ned would have avoided burnout through implementing these systems. Such a business would function effortlessly without his constant supervision even when fatigue sets in. Achieving lasting success forms the actual objective as opposed to mere achievement.

## The Art of Execution: A Human Conversation About Success and Spiritual Growth

Let's be real for a second. Many people achieve enthusiasm when they set goals yet these inspirations eventually disappear weeks after their initial excitement. Maybe life got in the way. Maybe you lost motivation. You used logic to validate the belief that you lacked readiness.

The true reality shows that you always possessed the readiness to begin. You just needed a system. Prior to dismissing the idea as typical productivity advice listen to what I have to say. The approach does not concern maximizing your daily work activities. Your true self needs your actions to match its values.

We need to explore this point through a personal interaction.

## Gather Your Resources First

The attempt to construct a house without both bricks and construction drawings leads to certain failure. Sounds ridiculous, right? The act of pursuing major life objectives without proper preparation matches the illogical nature of this practice. Make sure you secure your basic requirements including money together with tools and the proper people before starting anything. Think ahead. Before entering new territory research the subject. Prepare yourself ahead of time to avoid confusion while in the middle of your goal pursuit.

According to the Bhagavad Gita Krishna explains that Arjuna must first prepare his mind before entering battle. Preparation is power. The process of preparation protects you from internal disorder and stops you from being overwhelmed.

## Anticipate All Roadblocks Since They Will Definitely Materialize

Many individuals mistake starting a new project by getting excited and expecting everything to progress peacefully. The first energy dissipates as soon as obstacles appear since they will inevitably interfere.

When you consider the hurdles ahead during your first steps you would generate better resilience when they appear. Account first for resistance like the disciplined soldier of war conducts operational planning. You will view difficulties as game components rather than an indication to stop because you have prepared for challenges in advance.

The Book of Bible expresses this wise insight through its verse which states that foresighted individuals prepare for difficulties whereas unthinking people suffer because they cannot foresee upcoming struggles. The same wisdom applies here. Expect roadblocks. Be ready for them.

Creating daily operational practices surpasses the establishment of mere targets

Look, motivation is temporary. You can't rely on it. What you can rely on? Systems.

Daily systems through repetitive routines enable people to achieve inevitable success. The daily system stands as better than hoping that something will grow by itself.

**Stop Overthinking—Just Start**

## One of the biggest killers of progress? Overthinking.

People make themselves wait for ideal conditions together with ideal plans and ideal mental states. Gain some clarity by asking when you have ever encountered absolute perfection.

## Start messy. Start unsure. But start.

Lao Tzu taught that starting any journey requires only one fundamental step which leads to traveling 1000 miles. That's it. Just one step today. Then another tomorrow. You will establish something substantial by the time you notice.

Individuals must welcome frustration because it demonstrates their personal expansion

**Everything valuable in life** will eventually become uncomfortable at some stage. Every new skill and habit change as well as role transition brings uncomfortable feelings.

The sign of discomfort does not indicate stop but rather signifies ongoing development. It's proof that you're growing. The ancient Vedas explain tapas as the personal burning flame which emerges from voluntary disciplined action. When you endure, you transform.

## Your Present Self Will Gratefully Accept Every Decision That Leads to Personal Growth

### *Consider your situation twelve months ahead.*

Imagine looking back on today. Moving forward in life will bring you praise from future you because of the progress you make through challenges and setbacks.

### *Success isn't about grand gestures.*

Durability emerges through repeated little movements which compound throughout time. Set your systems. Anticipate your obstacles. Start before you're ready. The temporary unpleasant feeling turns out to be Your Hidden Potential at work.

So go. Execute. Build. If you experience a struggle remember to yourself that these difficulties belong to your path toward success. You've got this.

The discussion continues between us if this statement made sense to you.

### *Which system will you begin implementing right now?*

**Think about it .**

# X

# The Hidden Truth Behind Forgetting

Everyone faces the experience of name forgetting at some point but fails to investigate why it occurs. It's frustrating, right? You know you know it. The answer stays out of your grasp although you sense it nearby. Failure to grasp a name results in its faster retreat. Why does that happen?

Most people easily express their opinion that "Memory functions do this naturally." Names are hard to remember." This explanation succeeds as a basic explanation. Having enough time to process the matter reveals additional factors at play. The reason behind name deletions from our memory may actually result from an internal desire to forget rather than memory weakness.

Let me give you an example. At a moment during travel when having an everyday conversation your brain fails to retrieve the name of a well-known painter. When you make an attempt to remember the right name it produces wrong names which resemble the correct one but are not accurate. Weird, right? The moment your mind attempted to recall the name it encountered something else which grabbed its attention usually being an unpleasant thought or suppressed memory alongside ideas that brought uneasiness.

A mental operation operates in a similar way to evolving stream flow. The stream of remembering a specific item should remain uninterrupted yet at times a hidden thought emerges and disrupts the smooth recall. The name which you seek becomes trapped in this mental turbulence where an unexpected different name fills its place.

The occurrence of incorrect substitutions in your mind is not due to random brain errors. Such changes result from deliberate subconscious processes. Your mind often guides you toward different thoughts which prevent the emergence of emotional material that you currently cannot handle. The omitted mental objects could stem from past events or unresolved matters. Your brain uses this as a signal to refuse exploring a particular thought at the present moment.

These substitute names display a remarkable behavior that immediately appear in your thoughts. They're not random either. They're connected, just indirectly. When your mind redirects information it performs a deletion process instead of complete memory erasure. Your brain deliberately shields you from facing situations which it perceives as topics you should avoid.

You need to question whether forgetful moments occur more often because we are absentminded or because there is a hidden reason behind them. Our existence consists of numerous situations which get influenced by the ideas we actively try to evade.

All major religious texts including the Bhagavad Gita, the Bible and the Quran explain the nature of the human mind which tricks us into self-deception. Krishna describes the mind as "dirty, agitated, extremely resilient, and hard-to-control" in the Gita. And isn't that the truth? Our minds create belief in forgetfulness while retaining valuable information because a hidden force within directs the memory loss.

Remember to take a moment when you lose names because doing so will reveal more to you than you might think. Don't just brush it off. Take a few moments to remember what problem occupied your thoughts before you experience this issue. A hidden truth may present itself to your awareness. And who knows? This moment of awareness might help you remember both the forgotten name and the most valuable understanding about yourself.

The human brain occasionally loses the ability to remember names even though a person tries very hard. Your memory holds the name within reach of awareness but it escapes just like fog vanishes. And the funny part? Attempting to push it repeatedly only causes the name to disappear permanently.

Forgetfulness is not the primary cause for this inability. There's something deeper going on. Our minds do not exist in disorganized disorder. All things in existence carry purposes which drive their existence.

We have likely buried memories or feelings linked to that name that we wish to avoid.

We store these emotions that we choose to ignore even though we have hidden them within our subconscious mind. Our thoughts create barriers by guarding inaccessible places because the psychological process recognizes unexplored matters that cannot be handled at present.

This idea isn't new. The Bhagavad Gita, the Vedas, the Bible, and the Quran all touch on this in their own ways. Logic does not define us because we exist through experiences while keeping memories and displaying emotions. Our suppressed thoughts remain hidden within us until an opportune moment when they will reveal themselves.

# XI

# The Hidden Whispers of Forgetfulness

Do you recall situations when you were speaking with someone yet forgot the word you needed? Within your native tongue you are fluent, but straightforward words disappear from your mind without explanation. It seems to be an abnormality within the operating system. But why? Another word you previously heard could have set off a hidden thought because there were unexpressed issues or unresolved ideas involved. At that moment, you start to shift your attention without knowledge until your thoughts guide you toward a more profound understanding.

Our brains produce patterns during forgetfulness, which we usually fail to detect. It's not random. The human mind performs a transformation of occult feelings into quick blackouts where forgotten truths briefly disappear.

The idea affects our existence, so how should we interpret these revelations? It is essential to analyze what our mind wants to convey whenever we recognize instances of forgetting knowledge we should remember. What am I not seeing?

When considering all aspects, forgetting should not be interpreted as an absolute loss. Looking inward and listening for hidden messages and deeper meanings create opportunities through these instances of forgetting.

Every memory lingers in our minds, despite the common belief that things vanish from our awareness. The item exists in time until it receives proper recollection during its destined moment.

Do you remember meeting a person whose distinctive appearance stays vivid in your thoughts, although you cannot recall their name? The name eludes you, although it remains in the forefront of your awareness. Human memory behaves in surprising ways which feel strange to us.

The situation extends beyond the concept of memory. Our brains seem to possess a mechanism for shielding us against incidents which we are not yet prepared to encounter. The Bhagavad Gita, the Bible, the Quran, the Vedas—they all hint at this idea in different ways. Between us lies a mystery and the truth that you can unconsciously forget something deliberately. It's a signal. A subtle nudge from within.

Experience this discrepancy as you try to remember something before understanding that it links to challenging emotions you wish to avert.

The cause may stem from guilt alongside fear, as well as internal struggles that require resolution. Our minds force ourselves to forget specific details we believe will cause us distress because such information emerges unexpectedly in basic situations, including name and word memory glitches or missing recollections.

Forgetfulness as an experience happens for a specific reason and not accidentally. A single thread exists for anyone who chooses to track it. A name which fades from your memory stands related to distressing emotional matters. The improper use of a word exposes contradictory psychological elements between our desired perceptions and our deep-set fears. Our unconscious perpetually communicates unknown messages to us through an incomprehensible manner.

Consider a case of passionate discourse regarding justice, which includes discussions on the injustices inflicted upon one's people and the potential emergence of revenge-seeking descendants. At that moment, the speaker loses track of a word which should be effortless to recall.

Just blank out. Strange, right? Despite an inner pull toward change, to knowledge reveals a hidden reality about their psychological state which they do not actually desire the future they have predicted. Not all people are comforted by the concept of posterity because it triggers personal fear within them. A personal clash between fear produces momentary forgetfulness.

Memory functions as much beyond basic information storage and retrieval mechanisms. It's layered. It's alive. Our forgetfulness sometimes showcases inner aspects of ourselves that are greater than our recollections.

During moments of forgetfulness, pause your actions. Instead of frustration, try curiosity. I need to understand the meaning behind my forgetting events by asking myself this question. What am I not seeing? Things we forget often turn out to be those concepts we have not yet become ready to recall.

# XII
# The Echoes of Not Remembering

The human brain tends to lose some information while keeping other details in memory. Your ability to remember song choruses remains strong even though never hearing them again while important conversations and specific quotes impossible to remember. Funny, isn't it? But maybe not so random.

Take poetry, for example. The process of memorizing a young child learns a poem requires endless repetition until it remains permanently stored in their memory. After many years have passed you attempt to repeat the poem and specific words vanish while different ones substitute them. Why does that happen? Our memory tricks us or perhaps our subconscious wills something different.

A woman attempted to memorize an old poem however the words became disordered to her. The woman discovered that particular verse was dedicated to her romantic experiences from earlier times. Despite the hope she once received from this love relationship she became disheartened. The brain of this woman unconsciously altered specific text in the poem so the words expressed her current feelings of disillusionment. The story in her mind changed to fit her current emotional state.

Makes you think, doesn't it? How often do we do this? The way we modify our past experiences occurs through changes in memory that amount to anything but historical revision but rather creeps of forgetting and replacement and distortions. And more importantly, why?

The Bhagavad Gita presents the mind as both helpful and harmful to human life. The mind acts as our propeller for motion and simultaneously serves as an obstruction for progression. According to the Bible truth brings freedom but when our mind distorts transformative knowledge by concealing information then How can we be liberated? According to the Quran Allah avoids placing excessive loads on human souls so forgetfulness may serve as safety protocol. According to Vedas existence consists of Maya which generates the illusions that form our understanding of reality. The illusion may have forgetting as one of its components.

Your mind shows great discrimination about what details to keep versus what to discard yet this behavior deserves investigation. The forgotten phrases together with the misplaced words might be trying to convey a specific message. Our forgotten items remain accessible when we are ready to recollect them. The forgotten memories possibly wait patiently until we develop sufficient maturity to view them with accuracy.

Think about the reason behind any forgotten words or names or memories by asking yourself whether this could be standard memory failure or your soul delivering hidden messages.

You ever notice how sometimes a name just slips out of your mind? Like, you know you know it, but the harder you try to remember, the further away it feels? It's frustrating, right? But here's the thing—maybe it's not random at all. Maybe it's your mind playing a deeper game with you.

I've had this happen to me plenty of times. I'll be in the middle of a conversation, trying to recall someone's name, and boom—nothing. Just a blank space where the name should be. It's like my brain has temporarily locked it away. And sure, we could blame it on being tired or distracted, but what if there's something else at play? What if our minds are choosing what to remember and what to forget?

Let's say I meet someone whose name reminds me of a person I had a tough history with. Maybe I don't even realize it, but my mind does. And so, just like that, it buries the name. Not out of malice, but maybe as a way of protecting me from something uncomfortable. Our minds are always filtering, always deciding what's important and what can be set aside.

This isn't just me talking. If you look at spiritual texts—whether it's the Bhagavad Gita, the Vedas, the Bible, or the Quran—they all touch on the idea that memory isn't just a storage unit. It's alive. It's shaped by our emotions, our experiences, and even our subconscious fears. Krishna tells Arjuna that we're constantly shaped by our attachments and aversions. Jesus talks about how the truth sets us free—but sometimes, we aren't ready to face certain truths. And in the Quran, there's the idea that Allah causes us to forget certain things until the right time.

So, the next time you forget a name, maybe don't just brush it off. Ask yourself: Why did my mind decide to tuck this away? Is there something deeper here? Am I avoiding something, protecting myself from something, or maybe even being reminded of something I need to revisit?

Memory isn't just about recall. It's about meaning. And when we start paying attention to what we forget, we might just uncover something our soul has been trying to tell us all along.The Bhagavad Gita presents the mind as both helpful and harmful to human life.

# XIII

# The Power of Forgetting

A Conversation on memory, emotion, and the mind. Has it ever crossed your mind that the name remains just out of reach even though you are certain you know it? It's frustrating, right? The weird aspect of forgetfulness sometimes points toward a system rather than a chaotic process. When it comes to our thoughts they hide details from us in sly ways. Memories get buried in our minds although we remain diligent rather than unintentionally misplacing items since our unconscious mind is working a different layer below.

Think about it. Have you ever deliberately not speak a name because you fear that memory will resurface? Forgetting the name of something might stem from an ex-partner, a spot linked to regrettable events or simply age advancement memories. The name itself poses no difficulty for remembrance yet a hidden force within you stops yourself from recalling it.

Many spiritual writings starting with the Bhagavad Gita and continuing to the Bible along with the Quran and Vedas present forgetfulness as an essential component of a larger purpose. Krishna reveals to Arjuna that he stands as the fundamental origin of memory along with knowledge and forgetfulness. Think about that. Our brains naturally develop forgetting as a mechanism to determine our areas of concentration and which information vanishes from our minds.

Our emotions control which pieces of information we remember and what parts fade away from our minds in regular daily existence. During his Sicilian journey a male traveler loses access to the place name from his memory. Not a big deal, right? A realization hits him when he recognizes part of the name connected to veteran because he secretly avoids confronting his advancing age. His brain just blocks it out. The brain operates in a way that functions as a protective system.

The transmission of forgetfulness creates one more unusual situation. You are likely to forget something when a person poses a question about a person's name and then you start to forget their name during the same conversation. Our brains experience a system failure during this type of forgetful moment. Our brains harmonize with those nearby people who lead us to strengthen our recollections and erase our memory of certain things.

Take a moment when you forget something such as names or memories or locations. You should consider whether your memory lacks effort or if the situation demands further investigation. What we manage to put out of our minds happens to be avoidance of experiences we prefer to ignore. Remembering the forgotten things could be the path toward advancement.

## *Childhood and Concealing Memories: A Conversation on the Mind's Hidden Corners*

The significant experiences of our childhood development often fade into nonsense yet trivial memories remain fresh as clear glass in the human mind. It's strange, right? The mind stores unimportant information about first bicycles while it forgets meaningful experiences like a mother's comforting touch during frightful moments. Why is that?

Our memory functions through a picking process that decides between storage and discarding. The situation grows fascinating when particular mundane memories reveal themselves to be purposeful connections to deeper forgotten memories. They substitute forgotten deeper meanings through the use of ordinary everyday memories. Psychologists call these "concealing memories."

Think about it. When you search for a specific name recall your brain brings forth a completely unrelated word instead. Brain cells perform an exchange routine as they replace one memory thought with another. It's not a glitch. It's intentional. The same mechanism which operates on childhood memories functions identically in our mental processes.

During your youth you spent time in a garden while trying to differentiate between 'm' and 'n'. Seems innocent, right? You probably judged your childhood experience this way only to discover subsequently that you dealt with crucial life concepts simultaneously such as gender differences and ethical lessons and emotional states. My childhood memory about letters indicated something greater than written letters to me.

The Bhagavad Gita explains that the mind exists as both our biggest protector and our most significant threat. Our mind guards us throughout life yet simultaneously blocks important information from our understanding. According to the Quran Allah possesses the power to see the contents of human hearts despite human ignorance. According to Biblical teachings we can find freedom through truth but our minds usually block us from direct exposure to the truth. And the Vedas? Reality exists across multiple levels according to these teachings and the extent of our perception reveals only a minimal understanding of the greater reality.

The illogical memories of childhood serve as minor enigmas that our former selves purposefully created. These memories remain as encoded messages which we need to interpret.

Humans often lose most recollections from their early years to the point of forgetfulness. Experts suggest the human brain during early childhood lacked the capacity to properly save memories. The ability to remember things from very early childhood ages remains a mystery since some people have memories starting at ages two or three. According to some experts certain experiences with overwhelming or confusing circumstances make the mind create storage blocks for related memories. Despite the reason for forgotten childhood memories we have only these peculiar small fragments of real or altered or completely fabricated scenes to reconstruct our lost memories.

The following section concerns my individual experience. I had unexpectedly recalled a time when I stood sobbing in front of a wooden cabinet while believing my mother was trapped inside. The situation appeared meaningless to me at the beginning. Health professionals discovered that my childhood caretaker vanished when authorities caught her stealing thus learned that I associated that theft with being boxed inside a cupboard. His boyish humor described her as someone "boxed in." The idea of caskets in the conversation had a literal meaning for my developing consciousness. I developed exactly the same thought when my mother went away on that day.

See how the mind works? Our minds create meaningless connections between thoughts that slowly become clear when we analyze them from a wider perspective.

During your next recollection of an insignificant childhood memory please question yourself why this particular moment remains in your memory. Why now? Does the memory intend to communicate something important? We discover real truth through our suppressed memories instead of stored memories.

## *Slips of the Tongue*

Have you ever experienced a situation when unexpected words escape your mouth instead of the ones you wanted to say? Your words mean to say something precise yet you somehow end up speaking completely different language. Words often transform into other expressions that stand in place of designated names or verbalizations without warning. The typical explanation of "tongue slip" makes people laugh but does the phenomenon indicate anything beyond typical slips? The behavior of our spoken words exceeds basics of tongue slips. Does something profound influence our speech?

The ancient scriptures of the Bhagavad Gita, the Bible, the Quran and Vedas consistently support the idea that our spoken words do not arise blindly. Words and their absence as well as complete statements originate in profound inner places of our being. Every word we speak draws its origin from our mental concepts alongside our experienced emotions together with unconscious internal anxieties.

Everything we express through speech contains hidden strength according to the great sages of ancient times. According to traditional beliefs creation originated from a single word therefore why would the beginning so dramatically differ from the end?

Modern psychological experts identify this verbal error as a paraphasia which translates to brain failures in thought-to-speech connections. The unusual name may suggest a different explanation than accidental errors. The subconscious mind might be hiding an important communication inside our awareness. During brief instances, we might unintentionally disclose thoughts that we have not realized until that moment.

During a speech a politician approaches the microphone with the intention to start the session but declares "I declare this session closed." The audience bursts into laughter before he can adjust his statement correctly. Everyone laughs; he corrects himself. He could possibly wish for finality before this story had time to initiate. The mistaken words from the politician revealed an invisible truth that escaped through the spoken words.

The exact phenomenon frequently occurs throughout our regular activities. Has it ever slipped for you to call someone by their incorrect name? Maybe even an ex's name by accident? It's not random. Inside your mind this memory connection exists probably because of unexpressed feelings or merely past behavioral patterns. Either way, it tells a story.

Humans show systematic patterns when they experience forgetfulness of words. When looking for a name which begins with a particular letter you discover that your first thought was entirely wrong. Words that the brain retrieves go beyond purely logical retrieval because emotional associations together with unnoticeable psychological elements shape this memory function.

In ancient teachings the mind exists as a flow of water that keeps moving without end. Our mental processes bring forth thoughts both obvious ones and more concealed ones. Unexpected words frequently emerge during our speech moments without any warning.

Human tongue mishaps might not happen exclusively by chance. Mysterious slips of the tongue could possibly reveal aspects about our true selves. Our true identity becomes clearer to us through the analysis of our spontaneous words.

Have you ever spoken a word that sailed out from your mouth in a direction different than what you originally meant? The statements you are hearing shift mid-expression into unintended directions as though your brain possesses an invisible hidden message of its own.

Psychologists have been analyzing this phenomenon during multiple years of research. According to Wundt the mind operates in series of constant associations which flow like an unending river between sounds words and ideas. That flowing river stops intermittently. We possibly get distracted while we speak or suppress elements or perhaps we simply find ourselves unprepared at that moment. During this particular situation the mind makes an interesting decision to let insignificant details pass by.

Imagine this. Standing there you witness your child take a bite of apple which leads to facial expression and cut off impulse "The apel phony aspect appears as he gnaws on the apple" should be your remark. Your sentence begins with "The apel" instead of the expected "The apple." During such moments our brain creates an unexpected combination of "ape" and "apple" to generate an oddly modified word. A mistake? Sure. The mix-up in your vocabulary might reveal some hidden relationship between frustration or impatience as well as past apple-related memories.

A person mistakenly changes one sound of a word before they laugh it away. The small mistake might hold deep meaning which the subconscious mind tries to communicate. Maybe it's not random at all. There exists possibly a chink in the exterior which shows hidden truths.

The matter demands serious consideration which amazes all of us. Our words particularly the ones we stumble on reveal hidden elements within our minds. What the Bhagavad Gita suggests is that our mind can function as our best companion and our main enemy based on our level of mastery over it. People might realize they cannot regulate their thoughts to the extent they believe they can. According to the Vedas speech reveals thought patterns yet it might also indicate unacknowledged mental content. Words possess the ability to generate and destroy according to both the Bible and the Quran.

When you experience speech difficulties pause briefly to reflect upon what your mind might be sharing that moment. Perhaps your mind seeks to convey something significant. The random verbal mishap might not be accidental because it allows your subconscious mind to reveal thoughts you were not conscious of holding.

These slight slips will tell us something greater than mere verbalization. It's about what's behind them. Small communication blunders may be intentional expressions rather than actual mistakes.

Alright, let's talk. Not as some lofty guru, not as a scholar of ancient texts, but as one human to another. Ordinary people seek understanding within their thoughts along with the words they express including their mistakes because hidden powers direct them. This is all we truly are.

Has a blunder ever occurred where your words chose the wrong meaning without your awareness? Your lips intended an ex's name but released the name of your crush instead. On one occasion you should mention your love for your boss through your appreciation rather than professing your love. Embarrassing? Maybe. But also revealing.

What we mistakenly express by mistake without meaning to does not result from chance. Man takes shape according to his belief system according to the Bhagavad Gita. As he believes, so he is. Our subconscious beliefs along with suppressed emotions tend to escape facing downward when we least expect them.

My closest friend suffered a difficult end to her relationship. She swore she was over it. She drank her coffee and browsed her phone screen while constantly repeating "I've moved on." The habit of mistaking the name of her ex for that of her new fling would suddenly reveal itself during random conversations. Twice. Does the situation suggest your friend has completely moved on from her relationship? Her hidden emotions seemed to communicate things that her conscious mind did not want to accept.

Such slips receive analysis under the Freudian scientific approach. Through its verses the Quran describes nafs as the self which maintains concealed wants. According to Biblical texts the mouth shows what remains inside a person's heart because out of the abundance of heart content comes verbalization. And the Vedas? The human mind behaves like a breeze taking hidden truths from inside people into open display.

Even in the little things, the truth peeks through. One of her patients informed the doctor she had visited her husband for performance 606 but failed to remember the correct title was Officer 666. The real name? Officer 666. Small mistake, right? The medicine known as 606 functionally serves to treat particular diseases even though it represents both the drug and a rack number which led to their marital discord. Coincidence? The hints from her mind could have escaped her awareness while showing these truths to others.


And then there's money. A man entered a medical facility for examination before immediately stating he would wait before paying the consultation fee. Not pay, but play. What do you think happened? He never paid. His advancement of selfish motives became obvious before he actually committed the act.

Our words as well as our choices and mistakes expose our true nature to others. Not in a bad way, but in an honest way. People who want to grow aware of themselves should start by speaking honestly despite how uncomfortable it feels.

Pay attention when you mistake something because that small action reveals who you really are. A moment of pause should follow before you dismiss something as your mind needs time to convey its message to you. A hidden truth stands ready to become audible to others. During small insignificant moments our spirit reveals itself the most clearly.

When you speak do you ever realize that words escape you different from what you intended? The medical term is slip of the tongue though we refer to them as mistakes yet these incidents may not qualify. The heart likely knows what is shown by the mental acknowledgment of things.

Have you noticed the times when you address a friend incorrectly by their incorrect name or speak unintended verbalization? Our mind seems to display our hidden thoughts in such instances as if our subconscious attempts to express forgotten emotions.

The Bhagavad Gita describes how Krishna explains that human minds create their movement through constant shifting that resembles wind patterns. Biblical scripture says people express from their hearts whatever they bring forth in speaking. According to Islamic holy book the Quran our spoken words acquire meaning even though we do not grasp their meaning. And the Vedas? The scriptures admonish us that verbal expressions contain genuine insights despite our efforts to conceal anything.

The errors we commit while speaking truly qualify as mistakes? The errors we make when we speak potentially expose our actual inner thoughts to those around us. Why does a mother address her child with the name of another sibling? At her core she may understand them as parts of a whole linked through something that transcends verbalization. A young student accidentally calls himself with the title of his teacher during his initial meeting with the contrary. Embarrassing? Sure. The young man dreams of following the path that earned his teacher his status while hiding his true aspirations.

Humanity attempts total control over its statements as well as mental processes and emotional states within a world where we attempt to restrict every aspect. But our own words betray us. Not in a bad way, though. Our words seem to gently push us in a direction of facing truths we have been avoiding.

When you make a "wrong" statement stop for an instant before taking actions next. Don't just laugh it off. When faced with a situation ask yourself what mental message your mind is conveying. The truth may attempt to reveal something that you have dismissed. They might possess essential truth which requires being dealt with through listening.

Truth possesses an exceptional talent to evade secrecy it always manages to emerge despite our efforts to hide it.

People occasionally realize that their words in conversation reveal something other than their intended message. The words in your mind direct your speech toward one message but another truthful and genuine meaning emerges instead. Something in the atmosphere seems to prompt you with the secret that your thoughts already grasp even when your words try to conceal it.

We have all experienced these situations during conversation. You speak to someone while attempting to remain steadfast but suddenly a wrong phrase emerges out of your words. A moment later it becomes obvious that you have been discovered. Your subconscious mind reveals itself through carefully chosen statements which you were never aware of producing consciously.

According to the Bhagavad Gita both liberation and destruction come from the mind of a person. Our lack of self-honesty always results in eventual leakages of truth. A slip of the tongue? Maybe it's just that—a mistake. But maybe it's something deeper. What we genuinely believe shows through our words when we avoid acknowledging it.

During a public debate a debater strongly fights against one particular idea while completely disagreeing with it. The passion of the moment drives him to express opposition about something directly opposites what he actively opposes in life. Why?

A small indication exists that perhaps he harbors some doubt within himself. The conflicted part of his heart has settled on acceptance but his ego stands against this realization.

People who give advice attempt to project a balanced demeanor when they seek to look wise and collected. At the middle point of their speech they show their hidden doubts and self-contradicting aspects to the audience. The miswording is more than a simple speaking mistake. That's a mirror. The psyche of a person emerges from within to become visible.

The Quran declares that believers must avoid combining truth alongside falsehood as well as refraining from hiding what they know is true. Truth has its own mechanisms to reveal itself beyond our control. A slip of words coupled with nervous laughter together with incorrect words provide significant clues about someone's inner state.

The Bible features an instance where Peter terrified into denial claims three times that he does not recognize Jesus. His absence of love was not the reason. But his fear, his subconscious, overtook his words. A hidden struggle within him became visible through his lips. The crowing of a rooster revealed everything to him and he crumbled into pieces. Our spoken words occasionally reveal matters that we are incapable of acknowledging in that instant.

Pay attention whenever someone or yourself speaks with a slight mistake because the message extends beyond what words convey. Look beyond the words. What's really being said? How does the heart attempt to reveal itself through suppressed words the mind generates?

These apparently small flaws could turn out to be something else than mere mistakes. Truth is possibly searching to emerge from depths of people's consciousness.

People tend to observe their minds manipulating their thoughts throughout daily life. When you speak a certain thought you realize another idea escapes because it comes from a hidden level of yourself. Our culture describes this incident as a verbal mistake but actually it reveals truthful information through a mistake. But is it really? The truth slips through the safety measures we have established to protect ourselves.

Think about it. In The Merchant of Venice Portia discovers how duty clashes against her desires. Without intending to Portia reveals her love to Bassanio when she cannot help but speak her feelings. My whole self belongs to you and me both in equal parts which truly belong to me alone. The truth always breaks free from hiding even when we make intense efforts to contain it.

It's not just literature. We do this all the time. The natural impulse to admit hidden feelings surprises us when we suddenly discover we meant something different during conversations. Your ego ran behind your subconscious mind which delivered a message before it could catch up. Honesty becomes the potential reason behind that "mistaken" revelation.

Students of psychology also engage in spiritual exploration through the same self-exploration practices. Swabhava as described in the Bhagavad Gita represents our inner nature which attracts us toward our authentic self no matter how much we attempt to conceal it. The natural state of our essence always finds its way to break through every barrier we create to distort it or hide it from view.

According to Bible scripture: "The mouth reveals what exists in abundance within the heart." No matter how hard we work to organize our words the true essence of our soul manages to find its way out. The Islamic belief states that Allah interprets human inner thoughts before people express them verbally. The universe fully grasps whatever we believe we hide although we attempt to suppress our authentic self.

The revelation for us becomes clear from this discovery. These moments exist as signs to observe the essential feelings residing within our hearts. Mundane verbal mistakes and halting speech along with the spontaneous vocalizations that occur without time to modify them. Our true essence often finds a way to communicate precisely at those moments when we are not watching our tongues.

Listening would be better than dismissing such emotional moments. People are constantly trying to express their truth rather than having to battle to reveal it. Every one of us merely needs to halt our battle against this truth.

# XIV
# Missteps in Reading and Writing

Have you ever recognized the complete wrong interpretation of words while reading? When composing your words you sometimes leave words that deviate from your original thoughts? People usually dismiss these events as mistakes but is that an accurate evaluation? The errors in our reading and writing process might introduce incomprehensible insights into our thinking processes.

The abilities of reading writing and speaking function as more than robotic skills. Every mental output flows from the exact same internal source we possess which includes conscious thinking together with emotional and unconscious perspectives. All scriptures including the Bhagavad Gita and Vedas along with the Bible and Quran stress the role of mind power which determines what becomes real. Our minds occasionally deceive us through everyday incidents.

## A Misread Word, A Hidden Thought

As you browse through pages in a magazine while keeping it at a misaligned position your eyes unexpectedly register an unusual word. The original title on the page is A Wedding Celebration in the Baltic Sea while the title states A Wedding Celebration in the Odyssey. Without any warning your brain performed this unusual act and you found it funny but this incident left you questioning the reason behind it.

Your current thoughts concentrate on mythical accounts of historical stories especially relating to Odysseus in his travels. Your subconscious mind employs physical signals which target your unseeing conscious self for transferring hidden messages.

The experience mirrors the way our body signals a desire that our mind becomes aware of only afterward. The subconscious of a woman desiring children could cause her to constantly confuse stocks for storks. Personal fears may cause someone to misunderstand a written name to the degree of changing its entire meaning. Throughout our attempts to steer the boat the mind follows its natural course like a river.

## Slips in Writing—A Glimpse into the Unsaid

Writing mistakes function according to the same principle structure. When creating a record have you ever written an incorrect date either by advancing it or traveling backward by one month? Your thoughts at that moment may have focused either on anticipation of a future event or on dread while deeply lost in mental engagement.

The exact transaction amount I wanted to withdraw from my bank remained on my mind until I wrote the check but I accidentally added an additional figure. The initial impression was that it resulted from carelessness. At first glance it appeared to be a carelessness but then I understood it was the precise sale percentage that a bookseller had proposed for the books I planned to sell. Without noticing I had started evaluating possible financial choices before realizing it took hold of my mind.

Studies of unconsciousness by Freud revealed that supposedly unintended errors within the human mind lack randomness. Each small mistake has its foundation which includes subconscious desires and hidden thoughts and anxieties underneath. A brief reading or writing error delivers similar insights as dreaming when it comes to revealing subconscious wishes and fears.

## Why Does This Matter?

The short slips in daily communication involve much more than mere letter confusion or word misunderstanding. These small flaws appear as entry points which allow our true inner self to shine. Our inner self reveals itself through apparently random errors since we are more than just logic machines but also emotional and intuitive beings who surprise ourselves with their poetic nature when comprehending the world.

All divine scriptures emphasize self-awareness as the essential element for personal growth. According to the Gita there is a necessity for self-observation. According to the Bible we need to investigate what dwells within our hearts. The Quran instructs that Allah comprehends every hidden element we try to conceal from our own consciousness. Quick moments of carelessness in reading and writing tasks?

These missteps serve as life's guidance to signal you should focus and notice.

Look at your mistakes with presence of mind when you misspell or misunderstand something. Before you continue, please note down what thoughts enter your mind at that moment.

Keeping meticulous attention does not prevent minor errors from happening. A single word gets modified while a sentence changes direction unexpectedly which results in our original message transforming into an entirely new meaning. The absence of planned meaning arises during conversations together with writing and decision-making processes almost like reality includes minor mischief itself.

Think about it. During a speech a distinguished commentator tried to say their subject had retired in an unfortunate manner but an unintended art of silence in that sentence made the message switch in the opposite direction. The sentence transformed the mourning state into an apparent celebration of the loss. The wrong syntax for a negative statement led to this entire situation. The mistake makes me wonder if it was purely accidental since there seemed to be something more behind it. The real message somehow managed to escape through unanticipated wording.

Casual typos do not constrain these kinds of mistakes. A scientific book discussed star chemical elements in which the printed text showed "caribou" instead of "carbon." Researchers in the heavens searched for elements only to detect reindeer that became the final discovery. Such mind errors frequently occur in daily language use even though they seem illogical.

Such mental errors beyond common typos have even affected biblical text. A 1631 printing of biblical scripture omitted the one word found in the seventh commandment. The Bible demanded people to engage in adultery instead of prohibiting it through the seventh command. The printer spent a considerable amount of money due to a single typographical error. Money represents only one aspect of the problem since the confusion created by this misprint exceeded financial costs.

The interesting aspect is not only that these errors occur but also the series of factors that result in them. A woman composed a note to her sister to express congratulations about her new apartment which had upgraded to bigger dimensions. As she handled the envelope she misplaced her attention so she wrote down her sister's older and smaller initial home address. The woman displayed deep anger when she noticed the mistake because she seemed to resent her sister's expanded living quarters. Our unconscious mind expresses thoughts which we haven't freely spoken through such mental mistakes.

Freud identified these momentary verbal errors as "Freudian slips" yet all cultural traditions have been discussing the same phenomenon. According to the Bhagavad Gita the mind together with the senses proceeds ahead of conscious awareness like uncontrollable horses leading a chariot. According to the Bible the tongue will release whatever exceeds the content of our hearts. According to the Quran our hearts maintain an open connection between the inside and the outward expression of ourselves. In the Vedic literature there exists a discussion about subtle mental patterns known as samskaras which direct our thinking and behavior whenever we remain unaware of them.

So, what do we do with this? We should stop ourselves next time we notice ourselves making unintended statements through words or writings that astonish even our own selves. We ask for the deeper meaning rather than dismissing the situation because we seek to understand the inner workings. Honest words often emerge as our purest statements, even though we fail to control our spoken words.

# XV
# The Strange Nature of Forgetting

Let's talk about memory. The matter of memory proves to be quite complicated. We consider memory essential until a key fact evades our memory which we know we should remember. Memory suddenly behaves unpredictably as an untrustworthy companion who delayed arrivals or forgetful episodes or dangerous_hide_the_facts cases.

Although we can recall specific random memories from past years about atmospheric smells and car-listening songs we overlook where we placed our keys within the past few minutes. Our mind follows what exact process to select and retain information? The memory mechanism reveals itself through disappearances as well as unexpected reappearances and retained fragments.

People typically think forgetfulness occurs naturally through the same process as beach footprints disappearing. Research points to the possibility of forgetting existing as a non-random process. The decision-making process within our mind determines which memories disappear.

## The Selective Nature of Forgetting

When you recall the same trip with a friend through conversation their recollections show stark dissimilarities from yours. The fantastic sunset exists in their memory but it vanished completely from your mind despite being present at the same time. Why is that? What makes memories important cannot be defined by events as they occur. Your emotions along with subconscious decision-making powers determine what will be retained and what gets lost from your memory.

True memory loss is actually not a common occurrence because our mind somehow retains stored information indefinitely. Sometimes, they just get buried. When you have a dream your brain retrieves hidden memories that you had thought disappeared forever. Partial memories can sometimes emerge from the past during encounters with familiar odors and faces in addition to hearing special musical notes. The door in your mind silently emerges to display an abandoned space that escaped your memory.

## When Forgetting Isn't an Accident

Now, let's make it personal. Your brain triggers memory loss for unpleasant things that you dislike dealing with. A disagreement with someone you love together with an unpleasant mistake or an awful past incident that you wish to put out of your mind. Your brain neither loses nor ignores these memories but seems to deliberately stay away from them within its system.

I'll give you an example. My wife and I ate dinner at a restaurant where I faced an unwelcome encounter with a person I wanted to avoid. My wife listened to his friendly conversation with her own questions while my wife remained unaware of my past relationship with this person. It irritated me to no end. The strange fact ensued while relating this incident to my relative because I couldn't recollect a word of what he had spoken. My brain had erased it. I can't recall the things he said because recalling the memories brought up emotions I preferred to ignore.

The human brain makes this mental erasure process occur substantially more frequently than people might believe. The elimination of mental data involves more than memory loss since our brain functions as an avoidance mechanism. Our brain continuously edits our encountered situations to shield us from painful memories we wish to forget.

## The Mind's Quiet Tricks

The memory system shows another strange feature because some instances of forgetting result not from emotional states but from connected memories. Walking through a place generates a distressing discomfort although you cannot put your finger on what causes it. A familiar street you avoided during recent years and an understated store which seemed invisible through all these passing walks serves as two possible examples. One day you suddenly become aware of remembering a significant event at this location which your mind choose unconsciously to forget.

The search for a specific shop in the city dragged me all around the sector as I pass it regularly. No amount of effort would help me locate the absent place. I walked down each available street in the area without visiting the single street that remained hidden from me. It took me until I used a business directory to finally discover the exact location. The store existed within a building I frequented often before my friendship with my close friend deteriorated yet I purposefully avoided this area for numerous years. The street escape came naturally to me even though it did not stem from a conscious decision because some internal force had made that choice many years back.

## *Memory, Forgetting, and Self-Awareness*

So, what's the takeaway here? The human memory system operates beyond being an electronic device which stores files. Memory consists of an active process which evolves through emotional involvement and subconscious elements and unknown subconscious elements processing. The brain controls forgetting processes through mechanisms which exceed the definition of a technical failure. Sometimes, it's a message.

Our subconscious reveals hidden truths about our undealt issues through lost memories which also protect us from experiencing specific things. The process of self-discovery begins when we choose to give attention to what stays hidden in our forgotten memories.

Check whether the missing memory genuinely vanished when you notice information evading your recall ability. Has your mind hidden the memory or does it keep it safe to retrieve it at the correct time?

Have you ever experienced the feeling that lost objects are not truly lost as they exist somewhere in your environment? The item currently eludes you though it remains accessible because of a brief moment in time. Sometimes deeper inspection reveals that the specific object plays a minor role in the whole situation. That item reveals different symbolic meanings to users.

Take my desk, for example. People usually perceive my workspace as disordered yet I maintain complete awareness of all its contents because my desk shows papers and books flipping through various pages and a partially written notebook. I can locate every item inside that desk without any trouble. The discovery of my needed catalog's disappearance completely confused me. The author whose work I deeply respect had some pieces I wanted to purchase through that platform. His words always induce fresh perspectives to me. But guess what? I never found that catalog. I genuinely believe the truth is that I intentionally avoided finding it.

The disappearance of the catalog occurred possibly after someone commented on the writing's similarity to mine a few days before. The situation inside my mind began stirring unfamiliar emotions that I was unprepared to encounter. The writer I reached out to through a letter responded with curt detachment back when I was looking to connect. The fear of suffering another rejection caused me to avoid the situation where I might encounter something similar. So, the catalog 'disappeared.' Convenient, right?

A person I know previously kept distant from his wife while they lived together. No big fights, just this quiet distance between them. She made the thoughtful purchase of a book one day which she offered to him. A thoughtful gesture. Thanking his wife he placed the book away but lost it permanently. Months went by. During his observation of her tending to his sick parent he discovered a new perspective about her. That distance between them? The object served as an illusion because he had been holding onto it. He surprised himself by suddenly opening that drawer which revealed the long-lost book to him. The precious book stayed in its designated spot just as it had resumed its previous location.

The human brain manages unexpected things in amusing ways. People do not regularly lose things through misunderstanding. Our inability to understand certain things leads us to lose important items. The man behaves as if he forgot his suitcase keys despite knowing he does not want to attend the planned occasion. The smoking pipe experiences frequent disappearance whenever its owner gets caught smoking excessive amounts of cannabis. The seemingly coincidental occurrences between objects and mental lapses have deliberate purposes. They're signals. Clues to something deeper.

Object-related memory problems exist only as one part of the bigger picture. Do you experience cases where your mind destroys crucial information someone tells you? Have you ever perceived your brain switch itself off from comprehending a particular piece of information? That's not random. That's self-preservation at work. The human mind chooses to forget experiences which oppose our identity. Human nature has a habit of rewriting historical events without being conscious of this process. We chose not to lie as the truth remains uncomfortable to us.

Every time you lose something consider what genuine forces may be at work in your memory lap. Maybe it's just lost. Your mind may protect itself from information that it considers too difficult to process at this time.

Have you ever experienced an instance when you swear to remember something happening a particular way but later discover it is scientifically impossible? Today we will discuss the ways memory deceives us together with examining situations when our minds remember nonexistent events.

An enterprising but astute man was completely confident about having read about a book which didn't exist until after its official release. His strong belief was that he had encountered an advertisement about the book previously. Our investigation revealed the fact that such a thing was out of the question. Before releasing it to the public the book suffered complete silence in terms of announcements. So, what happened? Did his mind just make it up? Not exactly.

Brain functions differ from standard storage methods because it does not operate as a filing system. A storyteller is the better analogy since it puts random clues and fragments together to create something believable. Subconscious ambition motivates the man in these circumstances.

The young author of that book obtained his respect while simultaneously triggering hidden urges for him to produce similar work. His brain reconstructed the world around him to match the hidden wants inside his mind without his awareness. All people experience this type of mental rewriting in their own manner.

Think about it. No one is immune to forgetting essential tasks which pop up in awareness from time to time. The promise you made to yourself during morning light about sending the email later faded from your mind by evening so completely it vanished. That's not just forgetfulness. A hidden resistance most likely pushed the task from your awareness since part of you objected to completing it.

The lesson exists beyond theoretical boundaries because we witness real-life instances of this principle everywhere. In relationships, for example.

An important date or anniversary becomes forgotten to memory when someone does so. People tend to claim that memory loss occurred through mishap as the date seemed to fade from their thoughts. A crucial thing that matters to us cannot vanish in such a way when we are being truthful. Probably not. Their mind downgraded its importance on some basic level. They felt distant or there existed awkward emotions or their attachment level decreased after time passed. In circumstances of memory loss the actions manifest stronger messages than verbal declarations do.

And in something like military service? Forgetting isn't just forgetting—it's resistance. Order-related memory lapses by soldiers result from unwillingness rather than cognitive failure. The refusal to carry out the orders emerges from their inner opposition to what they have been instructed to do. The military system cannot accept the defense of forgetfulness because it detects this situation immediately. All evidence points to the fact that failure to remember something usually serves as a mask for reluctance.

So what's the takeaway here? Frequent forgetfulness does not necessarily indicate hidden contempt toward things you omit from memory. People realize much less about how thoughts and deeds connect to emotional factors than they believe. The mental process of fact retention transforms into semantic organization. People construct mental stories that fulfill their personal needs along with their anxieties while disregarding actual conditions.

When you face memory fog regarding something important it is worth questioning your subconscious motives. My mind attempts to express itself through this situation. Everyone would likely deliver an unexpected solution.

Human beings tend to forget things without any particular reason. Human beings disregard significant matters rather than simple things like key placement even though these matters should hold important value. Birthdays together with phone calls that needed a callback and those minor obligations regarding small assistance flow through our memory. Our minds seem to carry out internal rebellious functions that affect our memory capabilities.

Think about it. Your most essential things cannot escape your memory. No. The aspects of life which evoke a personal response in you remain fresh in your mind. And when you don't? At some level your inner self refuses to remember specific things because you really did not want to recall them.

Forgetfulness occurs accidentally according to the belief system which people defend as harmless. Our subconscious mind takes action to create clear boundaries between what we truly want and what we want to forget. The subconscious system aims to block memories of situations which we neither approve nor connect with on a profound level. Do you remember keeping a congratulatory message promise that later faded from your mind despite the time passing? The real reason lies in the fact that you lacked genuine excitement about the achieved victory. Our feelings seem to oppose the social pressures urging us to take certain actions.

We see this in everyday life. Several individuals have gained reputations for wide-ranging forgetfulness due to their frequent late work deadlines and total misplacement of everything they need to remember. Individuals express their forgetfulness by saying people are what they are stereotypically. Should this behavior reflect something beyond superficial aspects? The regular occurrences might demonstrate the actual order of importance that people choose in their lives. People would remember important things if they truly valued those things since forgetfulness does not happen with cherished priorities.

Have you noticed yourself delaying tasks that make you ponder about the reason for your hesitation? A type of delay happens that goes beyond normal procrastination involving postponing tasks until later. This resistance happens at a subconscious level. You recognize the important task in front of you but an unknown force stops you from completing it. Interestingly enough you cannot explain the reason behind it.

Procrastination contains an unusual element which transcends basic laziness and disorderly time adjustments. A mysterious force inside us works against us as we try to accomplish straightforward duties even though we have formally dedicated ourselves to completing them.

Think about it. People often forget their intended return time during tasks while planning to resume them in a few hours. The final completion triggers an awareness that you were actually containing some hidden resistance against the work. Maybe a small fear. Maybe a hidden reluctance. Maybe something completely unspoken.

Our minds operate in ways different from how we visualize our control of actions. Multiple unseen elements affect our decisions whether we carry out tasks or not. The real issue often stems from a nearby source rather than the task itself. You pause with an irrational delay during the task even though it will later unveil its reason for holding back.

It's funny, isn't it? Deep inside we understand that we avoided the task because we never truly wanted to complete it even though we made excuses about forgetting. A feeling of excessive giving combined with specific fears and an element of internal unrest toward the situation seemed to drive this decision.

Things begin to make sense when we recognize our resistance against something and ask ourselves what we truly avoid in that situation. We begin to understand hidden aspects when we stop pushing ourselves about things which require more than just time or effort.

Each time you put off completing something take a brief moment to halt your actions. Ask yourself genuinely why you delay rather than blamed yourself with guilt and pressure. My resistance indicates what it is that I should be exploring. A concealed revelation might appear before you.

# XVI

## Mistakes in Action – When We Get in Our Own Way

We believe we have absolute control over our movements yet reality proves different. Psychology—and maybe a little spirituality—tells us otherwise. Our subconscious feelings together with unexpressed desires and deepest thoughts insert themselves into our actions without our awareness.

A doctor who makes numerous home visits regularly finds himself accessing his house key at specific patient locations. He makes special visits to patients whose personalities capture his interest and who seem most open to reception. A mistake? Sure. But also, a quiet signal from his mind saying, This place feels like home.

The human brain leads individuals to attempt using their residential keys for office entrances in a way that suggests they want to be elsewhere. These things automatically happen to us without any conscious mental effort even though they occur regularly.

A simple mistake occurs when somebody takes more staircases than necessary during their journey. During moments when you concentrate on your ambition the body begins executing its steps automatically. Climbing higher, quite literally. You would discover this truth to yourself after reflection: You actually got caught in the endless pursuit to reach greater heights.

These brief lose of balance produce a sense of stern warning to the person experiencing them. A doctor at haste hurries past his exam room to pick a tuning fork instead of using his proper reflex hammer. Strange, right? When he pauses his thoughts he understands that the previous time he had used that tuning fork was with a child who completely focused on the object. An unconscious signal appears that causes me to question whether I am overlooking anything fundamental. His thoughts seem to recommend him to proceed with caution during this diagnostic process.

**Human** beings do not commit mistakes without reason. All human errors stem from meaningful sources including incorrect key placement and navigation mistakes and small mishaps. The human mind lets go of hidden intentions through unspoken thoughts or mental fears alongside brief moments which reveal your true inner thoughts. Such mistakes offer valuable insights to those who carefully observe them.

Observe yourself the next time you perform a mistake because one of these tiny errors. Your mind attempts to share its true message through these little mistakes.

Did you ever fall victim to a similar experience of accidentally taking something wrong? You extend your fingers toward your mobile phone only to feel the warm cup of coffee in your grasp. You attempt to retrieve your house key right before you reach the office entrance. Strange, right? Those seemingly small mistakes from reaching erroneous objects might have a more significant hidden meaning. The unintentional actions might hold a concealed meaning so significant.

Let's take a step back. A doctor enters his consultation having picked up his tuning fork instead of his typical reflex hammer. It's just a small mistake. A reflection makes him remember that he last used the tuning fork to produce sounds that held complete attention from a child. The doctor encountered his past mistake when a patient from years back returned with his medical condition much worse than it was during the original diagnosis.

Our subconscious delivers messages to us every day as our routine behaviors close around them. That doctor's mistake? There might be an intriguing purpose behind the thing he termed a mistake. A simple reminder seemed to have echoed inside his mind: Give careful notice. Don't rush. Don't repeat the past.

And then there's breaking things. Has it happened to you before to unintentionally drop something by yourself? Maybe a glass, maybe a favorite old object. Sometimes, it's just clumsiness. But sometimes, it's something else. A man accidentally destroys his inkstand just after his sister mentioned its unsynchronized appearance on his desk hours ago. It shatters. A coincidence? The inkstand's destruction might have sparked in his brain before his hand found the inkstand's location by accident.

These small indicators prove human beings never fully control their actions as we believe. Minds operate as vast oceans through which human individuals cannot follow all water movements. Situations when damage occurs lead to personal liberation. A quiet rebellion. A small sacrifice to unseen forces. Through this action the subconscious traverses into conscious awareness. I get it.

And it's not just objects. Has it happened to you that you uttered words which you never intended to speak? Accidentally naming your present love partner with your former partner's name? Awkward, sure. But also revealing. The mind maintains patterns, emotions and memories with a strength which people often fail to recognize.

Our subconscious mind occasionally reveals hidden thoughts through minor behavioral errors which we can label as Freudian slips. Our unconscious prompts us to pause reflection and contemplation about ourselves. Listening deeply will sometimes lead us to discover unrecognized aspects of our inner self.

Has it ever happened to you that negative sequences of events occur like they were destined? Your hope for internet disruption to get a break ends up with your router going down exactly at that moment. Coincidence? Maybe. Consider this statement for the duration you need.

The story from a teenage engineer left a strong impression on me. He along with his coworker were conducting a tremendously long experiment that usually drags down researchers through its mind-numbing duration. His co-worker mockingly proposed taking an early release after the machine malfunctioned but the engineer turned the valve incorrectly which made the whole experiment end prematurely. The engineer operated on a valve just as he had done one hundred previous times late in their shift. But this time? The system faced an overload because he received the pressure valve with its side facing the wrong direction. The machine broke down. Experiment cancelled. They went home early.

Funny how that works, right? The strange occurrences seem to match our hidden wants even though he claims it was unintentional. Deep within our psyche something seems to be paying attention and delivering results about what we stealthily desire.

Now, let's zoom out. Human beings experience accidental incidents such as falls and spills which end up altering our days unexpectedly with strange yet significant impacts.

Your absence from the train schedule led you to meet someone from your past. When your phone dropped maybe you paused at an ideal instant to detect beauty around you. People dismiss such occurrences as mere accidents although they may reflect unspoken internal thoughts we have not fully revealed to ourselves.

People find the situation increasingly intriguing during unsuspecting encounters with strangers as they continue in the same path thrice before stopping to exchange gazes. This situation represents an unfortunate accidental contact which should not be strange to anyone. Some fraction of human behavior reveals that we possibly obtain satisfaction from brief encounters during those awkward stops.

Serious mistakes which produce genuine outcomes often contain unexpected side effects. Medical professionals who have completed procedures numerous times maintain complete automatic performance. During that routine he blended a routine test solution with another random solution yet no harm was done. He notices that his entire focus had been on something unrelated to his present activity and unrelated to his present thoughts. The distracting thought managed to find its way into his physical actions.

So what does all this mean? The activities of our subconscious mind appear stronger than we actually perceive. Our thoughts may reach us through conscious awareness even if we maintain the delusion of being independent from mental processes. Stop and evaluate before making bad luck or neglect the cause for small errors. Check for any underlying factors that might exist. A mental suggestion leading toward something particular?

Life tends to create its own paths for us specifically during those occasions when we direct our complete focus elsewhere.

You may have experienced performing actions by chance that appear too specific to consider random. Your key search for misplacement happens exactly when you need to depart from somewhere you dislike. You let slip something during conversational missteps in exactly the unaccepted manner which makes you wonder if a part of your mind wanted the mishap to take place.

A respected doctor received a call to visit his uncle in critical health condition. This uncle maintained a dual role as the man who provided his upbringing after his father's death since he surpassed familial status. Despite knowing the end is near for his uncle the doctor comes running toward the hospital without hesitation. After reaching the scene he discovers the physician already finished his work while he had no input to offer at that time. So, he waits. And waits. His critical illness does not prevent the uncle from maintaining his grip on life.

The doctor checked his uncle's weak pulse during the evening and injected him with the treatment. He comes to understand he had selected the incorrect vial of medication. He chose to administer a lethal amount of hyoscine instead of the correct quantity of digitalis which proved to be his fatal error. His uncle dies within hours.

In this situation the logical side of the mind would accept it was a simple tragic accident. But was it just that? Later in life the doctor revealed he had concealed irritable feelings towards his uncle from himself. His young child lay critically ill at home calling for his presence even though he faced his sick mother in the hospital. The causal nature of this incident remains unclear because hidden subconscious forces might have been responsible.

This isn't about blame. Hidden emotions and old wounds and unspoken desires make our hands obey movements which we are unaware we are initiating. Can you recall the number of blunders you made while hiding essential motives from yourself? The missed deadline became accidental at the right moment to stop you from facing challenges you were unprepared to handle. You decided not to reply to a message that forced you to avoid an unease-filled dialog. There seemed to be a hidden plan that manifested behind the scenes.

Human beings perform this action numerous times in their daily routines. An account follows a female patient who suffered a leg fracture after her carriage accident. Upon closer investigation the event turned out not to be completely random. A strong argument emerged between this woman and her husband before the accident when he criticized her dancing as inappropriate. She chose horses on her own the following day and she did not permit her sister's baby to join them before experiencing continuous nervousness throughout the ride. The trouble arrived without warning as she leaped and ended up with a broken leg that left all others unharmed. She spent a long period resting in bed after her accident because dancing became impossible for her. She appeared to plan the very consequence she received from her husband's remark.

Humankind does not always plan to inflict self-harm upon themselves. But the mind is tricky. At times resolution proves to be so strong that your mind drives you toward a specific outcome which you secretly crave.

Human beings knowingly place themselves in situations that they expect to cause pain to themselves. People repetitively perform the same errors again and again. Certain accidents seem to lack complete accidental nature.

Take a moment to catch your breath before starting analysis on everything you've previously done. There is no reason to be fearful here because understanding represents being aware. People who recognize hidden forces within their behaviors gain awareness to intercept mental influences which could lead to later regret. When faced with unexpected incidents ask yourself both the basic facts along with their internal motivations. Which aspect of your being intended for that particular result? The answers might surprise you.

The term accident seems misleading because these situations rarely feel random. People call such incidents "bad luck" although they happen when someone handles a firearm that discharges harming them, their fate seems doubtful. People who stumble during moments of excessive guilt ask themselves whether that mishap was simply random.

A man told me about his devastating mood after ending up disappointed beyond measure. After he joined the military to forget everything the path became blocked and he chose to play with his revolver. Just playing, he said. Then the gunshot sounded and he received the injury. The gunshot wound prevented him from feeling completely at ease but did not endanger his life. He swore it was an accident. He failed to verify whether the gun contained ammunition while maintaining it in an ineffective hand position as though he was seeking harm without finishing the job.

This woman whom I choose to name Mrs. X appeared as a central character in my story. This woman who kept three children led a normal life as the mother of three. She stumbled while passing a store window where she saw a painting and hit her face on the wall. She hits the wall headfirst which causes her significant bruising. She dismisses the incident by attributing it to clumsiness although research reveals different circumstances. She only seconds before that incident had instructed her husband to maintain caution when on his feet. And before that? She had performed an abortion when she was younger something she now deeply mourns as she has concealed her feelings of remorse for numerous years. The body of the pregnant woman sent this message through self-inflicted wounds years ahead of natural childbirth.

Now, this isn't about judgment. Some inner struggles emerge when people fail to express their suffering thus making our behavior the outlet for venting this grief. The term "accident" might be incorrect since events seem like expressions intended to be noticed. Our inner selves sometimes attempt to express themselves through unexplained accidents that rise from deep within us. Trying to be understood? Trying, maybe, to be forgiven?

Our life gives us messages when we pay attention by ignoring random explanations rather than dismissing these events. There might be value in confronting past buried matters before they appear in different destructive ways.

So, what do you think? For some people there exist critical "accidents" which in retrospective seem to be expressing deeper meanings.

# XVII

# The Hidden Meanings Behind Our Actions

Have you ever observed that some of your actions take place without putting thought into them? Minor daily gestures and basic habits which people perform mindlessly include pen fidgeting and foot tapping as well as shirt thread pulling. Most people explain these incidents through randomness or boredom along with hand-related causes. These tiny apparent trivial movements from our bodies could possibly communicate an overlooked meaning.

Think about it. Have you ever cut your fingernails and after finishing abruptly remembered it although the injury was minimal? Maybe that fleeting incident brought something different than casual activity. A woman performs a sudden cut to the finger that should hold her wedding ring. Seems like nothing, right? When she performed this action on her marriage day it would become momentous. Now, that's interesting. A hidden reluctance along with an unspoken thought seems to bubble upward from beneath the surface.

***The human body reveals itself through words that escape conscious awareness.***

The act of ripping a hundred-dollar bill in two might occur to anyone without pause. Why? She discovers that previous inner turmoil regarding generosity toward charities together with showing gratitude to an outdated debt had been causing her distress. Her subliminal thoughts reached her behavior through an unconscious path.

We call these "symptomatic actions." The human mind sends these small unconscious messages through the body in a manner similar to minor leakages. Our body creates short signals from ideas that remain unassessed in our consciousness. All people engage in this habit. A person absentmindedly shakes coins inside their pocket. They are perpetually tangled in a small motion towards their sleeve. Little physical movements act as remnants from thoughts and experiences which remain unexpressed inside our psyche. The small physical signs serve as minute indications which reveal hidden meanings behind actions.

Among these behavioral patterns exist those which people perform repeatedly. People display two kinds of habitual behavior which include beard stroking during thought processes and finger ring spinning while feeling anxious. These behaviors do not occur by chance because they maintain important meanings. These patterns belong to each person since they show hidden aspects of their behavior which they do not recognize.

A doctor moved his office room layout by placing an antique wooden stethoscope between his medical chair and patient seating area although he had no specific reason for doing so. The instrument remained unused by him even though he wasn't willing to dispose of it. Why? He now understood that the object reminded him of his respected medical school mentor whom he greatly appreciated. The stethoscope awakened memories of doctors who provided him better trust than his biological father from his childhood years. He unknowingly established that stethoscope as a subtle protective symbol which connected him both in authority and assistance to his patients through the gap between their chairs.

So, what about you? Mental records reveal your habitual actions that happen without conscious thought. Have you ever found yourself in a brief instance wondering about your body movements? Maybe it's just a habit. A possible hidden part of yourself aims to convey a message through these motions. Something worth listening to.

Human minds tend to discover profound interpretations in everyday items which seem both random and meaningless. Humanity exhibits a peculiar mental process. Through observation we create mental connections that afterward affect our perception of life which determines the directions we follow in our lives.

The simple tool of a stethoscope functions as an illustration. A stethoscope serves as a medical instrument for most individuals. Watching their family doctor moving through the house with that small wooden stethoscope inside his hat created a magical impression on someone who grew up this way. A stethoscope functions beyond its purpose as a medical tool since it represents more than the sum of its parts. A bridge between knowledge and mystery.

When a young boy experiences the doctor's examination his breathing sounds emerge strong through the quiet as the wooden stethoscope touches his chest during the examination. The medical tool feels close to our bodies and produces a feeling of curiosity. That moment sticks. This mental imprint exists in the subconscious mind and the result is its transformation of thoughts and desires while affecting career path selections.

The medical professional can earn both respect along with envy from patients. Subconscious drives might be operating within some individuals creating a fascination for doctorlike power which phenomena resembles the presence of someone wielding authority in that way. The boy unintentionally matures into someone who desires the doctor profession.

Human imagination accepts symbols that enter into our nightly dreams and communications. According to Freud there exist no random phenomena which might prove his essential perspective. These three objects called a stethoscope as well as a sword together with a fountain pen exist as physical items to most people. But in the dream world?

They become something else. Between Sigurd and Brunhilda the named sword exists as more than just a sword. This object acts as a dividing line which shows constraining rules. The placement of a stethoscope by a doctor between his body and his patient represents more than an official medical protocol since it may function as a hidden balance between clinical need and sensual longing.

Every deliberate action we perform visible much more than we consciously express. Through absent-minded finger play with his bread the child produces a shapeless figure which reveals his true emotional state. Through this simple automatic action what psychological processes are forming within the unconscious of that person? The same behavior appears in someone who unconsciously taps their pen while dealing with mental struggles that stay unspoken. The mother whose hidden anger toward her opulent son-in-law ends up exchanging the medicine bottle with the jar of mustard in front of her husband.

People unintentionally disclose themselves through actions which they are not conscious of. When we make an effort to notice people around us we begin to identify their unconscious 'slips' revealing themselves more and more. An elderly husband and wife dining together show a case of food mix-up when the wife provides stomach medicine instead of mustard because of her diet restrictions. A mistake? Sure. The subconscious communication of the woman overrides her spoken intentions.

People everywhere carry personal symbols combined with routine activities or behavioral patterns which remain unknown to most individuals. Life offers a variety of smallest hints which bring a more meaningful tale when you choose to track them. Your awareness serves as the central point of this inquiry.

Humans communicate more information than they understand through their expressions both big and small. When a child forms a bread roll between his fingers he brings forth a basic yet unidentifiable shape while revealing his true feelings. Through that effortless and automatic action we can detect what emotions together with what ideas begin to form in the mind. People who unconsciously stick pens might contain silent mental battles similar to those expressed through the bread-fiddling child or the forgetful mother who reaches for the wrong bottle. A mother hiding her dislike of her opulent son-in-law makes a mistake by setting a bottle of medicine before her husband rather than the mustard.

People unintentionally expose their inner selves through habits they do not recognize. Being observant allows you to discover subtle accidental gestures in all individuals. At dinners with elderly patients a disciplined dieting wife provides stomach medicine instead of mustard to her husband. A mistake? Sure. This situation might reveal what her unconscious mind desires to express even past her deliberate statements.

We all carry personal symbols combined with habits and patterns which we know little about even though they express our deepest self. Throughout life we stumble across numerous hints which function as signs to uncover the bigger narrative behind them. You need to ask yourself whether you notice the signals around you.

Some actions of life occur without noticing unless we fully analyze them. During those moments you speak or perform specific tasks yet they feel like mistakes until you examine the situation fully you realize there is more. My tale can help you understand these unintentional incidents better.

One time my friend experienced an unexpected encounter with his philosophy doctor colleague. During lunch with his friend he discussed the problems that probationary students faced. Suddenly he disclosed that he obtained a top-level position as an ambassador secretary in Chile before completing his education. After the ambassador received his new assignment he chose not to introduce himself to his replacement. The man made that statement while eating pie but let the dessert fall from his hands at the precise moment of his declaration. The moment passed while he fumbled with his actions as though the incident was more complicated than average mistakes. Psychoanalysis holds great interest for my friend because he immediately recognized the underlying message.

He remarked that you permitted a choice bite to get away from you. The dropped pie served as a nonverbal indication that his co-worker intended to show his discomfort about facing both the new circumstances and the fresh colleague. He moved without notice between words and actions which perfectly matched each other. His ineptitude worked as an unconscious method to show hidden emotions he wanted to conceal. My friend pointed out the situation which led the man to instantly disclose how his lack of action resulted in the loss of that excellent chance.

We humans display this behavior in such a humorous way. Our powerful emotional state or hidden thoughts can force us to act unexpectedly without our awareness. A subconscious mental language expresses itself through us even though we attempt to conceal emotions.

Every one has experienced losing an essential item while thinking "I definitely did not wish to lose this valuable possession." Going beyond the surface sometimes shows that losing the object was not exclusively due to forgetfulness. The unconscious part of our mind seems to transmit a message through such situations. The same friend lost his most valued pencil just shortly after his brother-in-law sent him a severe written message. The pencil represented an old friendship yet he chose to free himself from that relationship through the symbolism of a gift even though he had no immediate thoughts about breaking it off.

A cook used to prepare a beloved pie for functions however during one occasion she brought it to the dinner only to bring it back toward the kitchen without explanation. She could not give a reason but she made it clear that she would never touch this pie even though it was her preferred dessert. The behavior resembles that of an unruly child who forbids their toy use by others only to become violent upon its confiscation. She did not remove the pie out of basic possessiveness but emerged from something more complex which she could not face within herself.

A huge invisible dimension exists within our daily movements once we step back to analyze the situation. We perform numerous unintentional or hazardous actions every day that actually transmit concealed meanings if we examine them thoroughly. These actions constitute an indirect form of both rebellious behavior and emotional management for suppressing internal struggles.

Every time we encounter small accidental events in our life they cease to be random occurrences. Our minds potentially use such actions to convey messages about what we may not have articulated consciously. Our subconscious deals with matters by expressing itself through little ordinary-but-significant actions that shout the strongest signals about our internal state.

People frequently face life events which initially escape their attention but afterward create significant effects. An unawares man enters the room without noticing my presence and places his coat over the seat which I planned to occupy. The man ignores the moment while his spouse gently informs him he has placed his coat on the intended seat.

My thoughts turned to all those instances when unintended actions spark confusion in others. Actions performed instinctively sometimes result in misunderstanding between people. The person on the receiving end? People tend to find hidden meanings in simple actions that we never meant to be significant thus creating awkwardness between us.

Human beings quickly develop interpretations from every situation they encounter. The person who committed the accidental error remains oblivious to what they did while others could perceive it as a blunder. Having no awareness of their actions they usually rebuff criticism since their behavior seems purposeless to them. The person experiencing the situation views it differently from the way the other individual does. The truth stands clear in front of the observer while those people remain unable to detect what you point out.

These individuals become irritated because they believe we misconstrue their meaning. The true nature of things escapes interpretation because intention seldom figures in actual situations. Being sensitive or perceptive about situations can lead to interpreting small matters in the wrong way. People who feel nervous tend to misunderstand one another leading to conflicts about minor matters.

We have reached the core analysis point. Being unaware while conducting actions creates a situation where we conceal aspects from our self-perception. Most people brush away things that cause tiny wrongs in their psyche though deep inside they recognize these deviations from state. You should face personal emotions when they occur since avoiding them leads to worsening problems. Humans carry out daily psychoanalysis sessions on each other though none of us recognize the process. Human behavior often leads people to observe one another intensely and beyond their ability to see themselves fully.

The investigation of our spontaneous behaviors when we observe ourselves leads towards personal growth. Knowledge of ourselves allows deeper comprehension of one another because of its reciprocal relationship. We should stop assigning blame for misunderstandings because all individuals possess unseen blind spots which might lead to better self-understanding by acknowledging our occasional mistakes.

An analysis of unnoticed mistakes is our subject for today. Sometimes you think you know something completely but your mind creates uncertainties about what your memory stored. Your mind appears to trick you without your awareness of it. The misremembered information can be crucial in nature.

The information about the birthplace in my research paper contained an inaccurate memory which stemmed from a dream. I made a mistake on the city where the figure was born despite knowing the real place which only surfaced in a dream. The moment I awoke from my slumber I possessed a freshly generated recollection that contrasted with the previous vision about the book. Although I firmly knew the city where he was born. What reason did my thought process have for providing a different version of reality? The puzzle piece somehow vanished on its own since my brain seemed to conceal it from me purposefully.

This happens all the time. Our brains silently work in the background since we focus on something else by rearranging memories until they deliver wrong information at untimely moments. These occurrences in the human mind are not necessarily honest mistakes. Inside you exists something which seems to work against seeing real truths. The strange phenomenon appears randomly through unfamiliar place names one has no reason to recall.

I actually misinterpreted that historical fact later on. The wrong information escaped from the depths of my mind intentionally. It had a deeper meaning. The suppressed memory which I tried not to face brought forth the mistake through something trivial I failed to notice. My brain developed an alternative version of events after I chose to push a specific memory of my father into the depths of my mind.

Every person participates in this method despite being unaware of it. All people choose to hide their emotions together with their forgotten past experiences as well as those matters they seek to ignore. Our suppressed thoughts always find a way to reappear because they sneak back into our minds through our decisions and behaviors and mistakes. Our mind attempts to safeguard us from something by corrupting factual information.

People naturally possess an unconscious part of themselves which they prefer to keep buried in forgetfulness. Unexpected circumstances allow unexpected memories to enter our everyday life as they appear through name forgetfulness and distorted memories and minor mistakes. We can learn important things about ourselves when we focus on the unintended blunders which occur naturally. Somewhere in the confusion lies a truth that matches the way errors surface within our lives.

Do you spot your mistakes when they happen through verbal or physical errors that make you understand something bigger than an error is operating? Some hidden force operated in that incident which transformed the mistake into a deeper meaning beyond accidental intention.

The experience has happened to me. When I promised the patient two books I entered the library with good intentions only to discover I brought him the incorrect titles. It became necessary for me to accept that the situation extended beyond simple error. I seemed to deny myself consciously from providing him the books maybe because I disagreed with his travel intentions. I realized too late that my fabrication had been a mistake when the time came. And guess what? The whole situation shifted beyond the books to the way I attempted to conceal my actual emotions.

It's strange, isn't it? These common everyday scenarios trap us when unexpected events occur but our minds fleet to the question of whether these incidents exceed simple forgetfulness. Our habit of following what appears to be right has trained us to neglect self-checks with genuine emotions and real truths about everything.

One of my patients had a breakup planned for his girlfriend yet called the love interest instead of me during his therapy session. He telephoned his ex-girlfriend rather than speak with me in my professional capacity to ask permission to use my name. It wasn't planned. Although the mistake was honest there seemed to be something inherent about his emotional disposition regarding this matter. His subconscious voice suggested that he wanted to avoid the breakup despite his rational thoughts which supported moving forward.

These mistakes occur regularly within all people and especially surface whenever we perform a task that brings us no satisfaction. The trip to my brother's English residence became a complicated series of directions both literal and figurative. My journey transported me to Holland when I meant to arrive in England. People may initially view this incident as a pure accident but the evidence rejects this claim. The trip was supposed to be brief but my subconscious may have been pointing me toward Amsterdam art galleries since I had long desired to see them.

Mistakes appear independently from each other. These little separations in your experience allow you to examine what is growing inside your heart as well as observe your true nature. These setbacks point to important hidden matters we want to ignore or they possibly symbolize our lack of conscious control.

Everytime you spot one of your missteps you should make the effort to understand the root cause. Pause and think about what actual factors exist within this situation. My mind might be attempting to convey some crucial information to me at this point. Our wrong choices might stem from lack of agreement between our genuine desires and beliefs.

Everyone dances their minds toward understanding both the world and their personal position within it. The truth emerges as an unintended consequence of life's chaotic events which are messy rather than neat. But maybe that's the point. Small mistakes might be the exact fragments which need our attention the most.

To better understand this idea we should examine it through regular human experiences. When life sends these minor events that turn out to be bigger indicators of our situation than we expect. Have you experienced forgetting about a task after concluding you did not require its completion? A concealed power acts against your efforts to recall things which you try hard to remember.

My friend experienced such a situation which I will share with you now. The literary society had no appeal to him since he joined despite his dislike yet hoped membership would improve his playwriting craft. He began by being focused since he attended all gatherings in the beginning. His life changes completely after he receives news about his play being chosen for theater performance which eliminates his interest in those society meetings.

Time passes during which he gradually forgets about them although he intended to remember. He battles feelings of shame since his forgetfulness makes him believe he has failed others although he reassures himself stating "I will remember next Friday." I swear." He arrives at the meeting room door on that day with strong determination yet discovers that the door is already locked. The gathering came to an end because he attended it on the incorrect day. His memory failure seemed more than forgetfulness because the universe seemed to assist him in forgetting.

This other story exists equally as remarkable yet amusing in its nature. A woman accompanies her artist brother-in-law during his travel to Rome. During his stay he received a magnificent antique gold medal that German residents generously bestowed upon him. The gift recipient fails to display enough gratitude which leads her to return the present to his possession.

When she arrives home she finds to her surprise that she has secretly managed to keep the medal with her. It's just there, in her bag. She decides in her mind to send it back to its owner the following day. But the medal keeps disappearing.

She looks everywhere but the gold medal remains lost to her. She eventually understands why the medal never left her possession: she had always wanted to keep it. The choice to keep the medal was not due to chance but rather emerged from her subconscious mind.

The story follows Jones who possesses a letter he insists on sending although he constantly forgets to post it. The letter which he should send out remains in his possession as he continually fails to complete the postal task. He keeps the letter resting on his desk until the days stretch into multiple ones.

Jones sends the letter without a destination after posting it which results in its return by the Dead-letter Office because he omitted address details. Following the missing stamp correction he proceeds to forget stamping it altogether. It comes back again. His thoughts about desiring to send the letter do not seem accurate with his subconscious avoidance behaviors. Has life ever pushed you to carry out a plan only to find each movement facing brutal obstacles in your path?

The realization hit him that his friend had not paid him back for the money owed to him since the friend seemed unlikely to recover it in the near future.

A series of other tasks drew his attention after he wrapped the book and left it on his desk. The passage of time made him recall the book too late because he had already parted with it. His mind fought against performing a task he disliked although it could bring positive results.

All these stories carry a deeper meaning than forgetfulness because they reveal concealed desires and shadowy motives within human nature. Most people have hidden desires which contradict their initial thoughts and desires.

Those concealed yet delicate forces determine our actions more than we are actually aware of. Our minds send us into a specific path before revealing that we have followed a totally different direction from the start.

To understand why you forget something seek an explanation especially when you detect your deliberate avoidance of something you believed you wanted before. Beyond the natural nature of forgetfulness might be an underlying reason that permeates memory functions.

Have you ever repeated the same error continuously without comprehending what causes it? The universe delivers its message of repetition to you through indirect means until you make time to understand its purpose. A recent story I encountered depicts these principles about the subconscious mind that operate behind the scenes.

A man demonstrating absolute neatness habits All his affairs are perfectly organized which makes him appear very exacting in every manner. During his outing he checked his watch before realizing it had vanished permanently.

Never happened before. The situation makes him feel confused although he stays stable and unpanicked. The man must keep his appointment and requires a watch at the moment. The man took a watch from his friend saying he would give it back the following day. The situation seems straightforward for everybody else.

On the following day a surprise occurs. He makes the mistake of leaving the watch behind him when he leaves. His own wristwatch serves him well yet he still possesses her wristwatch. His watch remains at home while he carries out his regular activities. He senses something is off because he seems unable to handle this situation which controls him.

He attempts once more because he wants to resolve this situation. After reaching his friend's location he observes her then a forgetful incident occurs. He accidentally leaves behind his own wristwatch after visiting her house. The situation has transformed into an uncontrollable loop from which he cannot get free.

He questions himself by asking why these two forgetful incidents are occurring. His habit of not forgetting things differs substantially because this essential watch is a strong deviation from his usual behavior. The deep consideration leads him to have his understanding moment. Before his departure from home he spoke with his mother about some matter.

His mother revealed that his problem-causing relative who stole his watch demanded additional funds to retrieve it from the pawn shop. Everything became clear to him when this revelation struck him with intense force. Each accumulated feeling of mistreatment along with experiencing disempowerment toward others came flooding back to him.

When faced with expressionless rage he could not articulate his resentment to those who exploited him his subconscious mind discovered this behavioral outlet. Money had become an issue that he refused to give to that person anymore. His mind made the decision switching off his watch without his knowledge to take it.

He decided to hold on to his watch as it embodied something crucial he neither desired to surrender nor abandon. This action served as a tiny rebellion because he wanted to push back against his feeling of being exploited. Despite his deliberate attempt to give back the watch he still could not manage to do it. Something inside him prevented him from turning over the watch. The mixture of his fury and powerlessness forced him to maintain possession of the watch even though it belonged to someone else.

The power of unconscious decision-making becomes evident from this particular example. Most people believe they control their actions but things are different at an unconscious level. Realistically human beings generate unconscious choices our conscious minds remain oblivious to. The watch kept his possession beyond a simple memory default.

Somewhere within him he held onto one thing—the watch or the possibility of seeing his friend once again by pretending to return a favor. The watch held personal value to him because his life was dwindling away.

We can see ourselves and our feelings better by looking at the small forgetful incidents we experience in our daily lives. Our minds may dismiss what we forget as usual forgetfulness yet deep down we recognize we are ignoring issues we do not want to face. Our brain uses memory lapses as a defense mechanism to escape from overwhelming pressures which have persisted for an extended period.

Whenever loops of repeating errors and forgetful moments occur you should check beneath the surface of things to understand your real inner processes. What's the deeper story here?

Have you ever experienced a series of failed attempts while trying to achieve the same thing repeatedly? You may wonder, "Is there any way to understand this?" Later when you reflect on such occurrences you discover they are no mistake. The hidden aspect of your personality directs you toward farsighted decision making without your conscious knowledge.

In a certain situation a man repeatedly loses his watch yet remembers to keep forgetting the watch of his female companion. At the beginning he was unaware of what was happening but exploring the situation cleared up his understanding. The incident looks like merely a small misstep to most people. The deeper meaning behind this situation could show that he was handling an internal struggle. One aspect of his character rebelled against two watches because he considered it both excessive and shameful since he wanted to help his family member.

A symbolic meaning appeared to exist in this moment. The man aimed to fulfill his familial responsibilities and keep an eye on his romantic feelings toward this woman.

The matter deepens into an even more profound issue here. There's another layer. The person suffered difficulties displaying the female watch publicly. The situation made him uncomfortable because as a bachelor he had to show his friends an explanation about carrying a ladies watch. The entire event felt wrong to him because he believed he was breaking a fundamental rule of being a man without the support of being independent. His unconscious intelligence chose absolute forgetfulness over the watch as a simple solution to resolve the dilemma. A solution through continuous thinking about the watch made him face yet another issue. He needed to bring the watch back while his thinking process navigated the complete maze between his emotions and responsibilities and his wish to dodge arguments.

Our assessment moves into profound levels because you can't interpret this as a case of forgetting a watch alone. The unconscious mind reveals hidden truths which lie beneath our level of awareness even though we remain unconscious of them. All little mistakes we make exist without randomness in their order. These signs act as warning indicators to point toward subconscious matters that we avoid facing directly.

Take me, for example. During one night I dreamed of losing my entire wallet so intensely that I woke up to discover my pocket actually empty. It felt so real. After waking up I checked all my pockets then shock when I discovered the wallet actually vanished. The discovery made me recall the exact moment right before going to bed when I had left the wallet where it was staying. The wallet loss stood by itself as the core issue. My subconscious signaled that I was seeking to harness and confront one significant emotional matter I prefer to ignore.

Small mistakes usually link to significant emotional or psychological issues that we face. Our brain attempts to alert us while using methods that make it difficult to disregard. People struggle to control this phenomenon intentionally yet they end up performing the very action which they intend to avoid despite all efforts. Why? There exists an inner force which directs our actions. The motive that drives a behavior stands more important than the behavior itself.

Take a quick moment before you move forward whenever you forget important things or complete unnecessary repetitive patterns. The underlying connection might be making an attempt to reach your awareness. Your mind attempts to communicate distinct information even though you seem unprepared for it. Unconscious choices appear to be mistakes because our brain pushes us toward the deep truths we are ignoring subconsciously.

The main idea is that our thinking and actions appear to have control like they do although we prefer to believe so. People believe their decisions stem from conscious selection however unconscious forces may control what we genuinely select. Human beings might not have the level of independence they believe they possess. The main challenge becomes apparent when people observe such items yet choose to disregard them or make random chance explanations. These so-called errors often reveal key messages from your internal self which aim to get your awareness.

Humans need to reduce their speed to recognize these instances. These instances reveal themselves to be less random than they initially seem to be. The universe possesses a natural ability to guide us toward directions that we are unaware of noticing. Our little mistakes may intentionally guide us toward understanding that our thoughts are more meaningful than we could currently realize.

Before dismissing something be mindful to ask yourself what meaningful messages lie behind forgetfulness or verbal slip-ups or strange insights. Something beyond your basic awareness might be directing your path although your current awareness remains unaware of this process.

Our minds occasionally receive numbers from life's daily flow or we unconsciously develop fixations toward numbers so we naturally perceive them as random random thoughts. Have you ever away regarding hidden forces possibly hidden beneath numbers? Please continue through this seemingly unorthodox passage.

Random numbers should only lead us to consider their possible interpretations about our personal situation without excessive speculation. That number which continues to repeat itself in your consciousness along with those irrelevant flashes of thoughts might be delivering valuable information about your personal journey through life.

Life presents itself as a humorous experience which we can agree upon. People execute these routines while preoccupied with their next movement because they think the purpose is reaching the destination. But sometimes, it's not. A few things we learn about ourselves can appear in unexpected moments such as random thoughts or brief experiences. We may not recognize these insights we are starting to receive at this time. Our unconscious mind seems to compel us to face aspects we have been alienating ourselves from.

Pay attention to the numbers which appear to you in your thoughts or surprise unexpected thoughts which emerge because they could hold vital information about your life. The clue could possibly showcase hidden layers within yourself. You seem to have a puzzle hidden in your current situation or in your personal history or your future direction that remains a mystery to you. Everything links together despite the initial concealed nature of these connections. Thus the entire concept might be what makes it enjoyable.

We should discuss the critical turning point which causes confusion when your thoughts start doubting all facts. Have you ever been there? You encounter critical choices where you cannot determine your following course of action. It can be frustrating, right? Your diligence and accomplishments throughout life meet challenges because your mind asks if you possess enough capabilities for upcoming opportunities and doubts whether you follow the proper direction.

I was in a similar spot once. I completed my work at the state hospital where life had been prosperous. All the accolades and recognition points were satisfying in the papers I held. Inside me I sensed there ought to be a different direction in my life. Having learned your training job it finally sets in that the way forward differs from your personal direction.

Movement and starting my career in private practice alongside marriage were the objectives I kept in sight. The nagging question haunts me as I wonder about my ability to do it. Modern times no longer offer stability because the existing patterns and structures to depend upon are gone.

The progress made in mental health treatment since my time in school still caused hesitation regarding my ability to properly treat actual patients with serious emotional challenges. I devoted all my practice hours caring for controlled patients yet doubts entered my mind regarding treating outside the standard patient demographic. Would I be enough?

Do I have the capability to assist them properly or would sending them to a larger facility be the right solution? Someone has genuine anxiety regarding this scenario. The deep concern emerges when you wish to assist yet doubt whether your competency level is sufficient. Remaining at the cliff's edge you can only see the unknown forward.

During my visit to Paris I shared a matching psychological state because I thought fresh surroundings would resolve my problems. I visited that location without discovering answers to the questions on my mind. The current mental health approach to fixing damaged components using patchwork methods left me dissatisfied.

Deep understanding along with the fundamental essence of the work seemed to be missing completely. It was discouraging. A change in my professional direction began to cross my mind. The decision to abandon mental health as an answer for myself became a possibility.

But then, a letter arrived. That single piece of writing carried the strength of a life-saving link toward me. A trusted mentor who had previously guided me sent me a guiding message. He encouraged me to leave for Zurich and continue my studies of human mental functions through intense research. And suddenly, everything shifted. His single piece of guidance made me recover my belief that psychiatric studies might truly be within my reach and not so impossible.

It's funny, isn't it? A single straightforward thing transforms our entire life path. Sometimes we lose direction when we wonder if we possess the abilities to handle upcoming challenges. Small guidance through letters and conversations alongside new ideas will take us directly to what we need.

My return to the psychiatric field began with a new passion to explore psychiatry which I integrated with valuable new perspectives.

The self-reflection phase brought me this unexpected experience. I experienced a deep realization at that moment which was significant. I discovered this awareness because my experience revolved around unnoticeable realizations rather than significant life decisions. No one in the faculty catalogue contained my full name despite only using my name for identification.

A small thing, but it stung. All the unobserved basic aspects of life suddenly popped into my awareness because they kept falling unnoticed though we feel entitled to them. People struggle to obtain recognition although reality sometimes fails to recognize their worth. It's frustrating. Being overlooked in the faculty listing became yet another part of my educational journey. You need to establish your position while society fails to acknowledge your accomplishments.

In simple terms understanding reveals that most of our difficulties do not happen by chance because they link back to unexpressed aspirations. The things we truly desire yet have not materialized drive all our life experiences. Life provides information about directions only occasionally instead of presenting complete guidance at every turn. With adequate investigation you will notice patterns which link various elements like puzzle pieces moving into precise positions.

Many large answers to our crucial questions often prove simpler than what we had anticipated. The true revelation about life often surfaces through everyday simple situations although they seem inconsequential. A personal discovery happens when someone we trust encourages us through their guidance or when we become aware subtly or through a forgotten memory. Our existence demonstrates unexpected progress while appearing lost because we are continuously advancing in life.

Have you ever considered that our automatic mental and physical actions can expose inner spiritual aspects about ourselves? Has your mind performed background activities that remain unfamiliar to your first understanding? The subtle voice inside our mind points out how we unexpectedly carried out certain actions. A few individuals strongly focus on tiny matters that seem unimportant to normal human responses.

For example. We all have encountered someone who interprets ordinary things as major signals during our lives.

A quick glance followed by a single gesture or the way someone grips a drink usually makes a person see complex schemes or symbols where there are none. People today frequently believe they notice hidden elements that others cannot perceive yet without realizing their minds create mental illusions from their inner thoughts. Such individuals perceive internal thoughts and mix them up as external reality.

My statement does not dismiss every single observation reported by such individuals. People maintain some truth even in their fabricated scenarios because we naturally have gut feelings which signal events that are about to happen. Our unconscious mind creates these connections even though we remain unaware of them which avoids any magical yet false assumptions.

We begin to see problems when we believe everything is linked together with deep significance because this leads us into a complex situation. This experience involves understanding a clearer vision which probably does not exist.

Superstitions become intriguing because of this phenomenon. Would you ever find yourself doing the following thought process: "This seems unusual. Maybe that means something?" The experience of discovering the wrong house entry during an unexpected bump against someone becomes an apparent universe message.

When I was hurrying to visit a patient the taxi brought me to an incorrect house address. Under superstitious thinking that situation would signal a bad sign because it was a warning. The wrong place turned out to be nothing more than a simple mistake according to me.

Haste created the mistake during this incident. A superstitious individual creates significance from each minor encounter that happens to them. The superstitious person would transform this unintentional route deviation into a supposed message about what is ahead.

Is there any distinction between you and me? I understand everything in life exists by chance and the world progresses without my need to interpret every passing moment. Each thing in their life seems to represent a significant meaning. Both groups wish to understand chaotic surroundings yet they seek their meaning externally versus internally. Why do we do this? The working mechanism of our unconscious brain creates a constant pursuit to find order within the world even when there may be none.

Your brain creates mental safety mechanisms so we substitute unknown information with personal interpretations stemming from our biases in order to find meaning. Take superstition, for example.

Fear that we have suppressed over time transforms into superstitions. Our behavior functions as a natural protective response mainly because we have unconscious ideas and negative impulses whichautoreleasepool.

While it remains simpler to focus on external factors for negative fortunes we avoid confronting the reality that we potentially contribute to our adversities.

We need to question whether genuine elements exist within the series of so-called accidents. These odd occurrences and emotional sensations could be showing us secrets about reality although we exclude magic and destiny from this discussion. What if they're not random? Certain experiences including dream visions and sensations from our gut match reality so precisely they cannot be dismissed. Whenever we experience these events we need to evaluate how much our brains created these perceptions and how much the universe intends to communicate with us.

I cannot establish certainty about it. I have not experienced any major mystical revelation but I did have random occasions where things connected in ways that could not be explained through regular reasoning. As we explore the mind we discover its immense mystery because it contains unidentified thoughts as well as desires and fears that are slowly becoming known to us. Each sign or coincidence leads us to wonder if it symbolizes something transcendent. Everyone has their own freedom to determine this issue.

Whenever you face something unusual or notice subtle indications from the universe consider briefly questioning whether these signals have genuine meaning. My thoughts might be working to understand the world in their distinctive manner or these experiences may truly exist.

Our interpretations and understandings of everything depend on our perspective toward worldwide signals. Maybe behind our current understanding sits much more than we are presently aware of. Knowledge points beyond our current tier of observation so we need to study our own emotions and instincts more deeply.

The way our life operates at times produces an inexplicable combination between unusual thoughts and meaningful coincidences. Life presents those moments when activities touch our lives in a feeling of too strong a connection that seems significant. When you focus on someone in your mind the person suddenly appears or their name pops into your hearing. It's weird, right? Random coincidences may dismiss as mere accidental events although the situation might demonstrate something deeper.

A single instance occurred in my life which felt peculiar. While strolling down that street I observed a pair of romantic individuals some distance in front of me. The couple approached without my notice but when I reached twenty steps away I realized they were familiar somehow. This knowledge came silently without any obvious sign rather through personal recognition.

At this fleeting moment your mind remains between sleep and full consciousness thus noticing things without total awareness—like an obscure thought suddenly arises. My emotions seemed to take over randomly since I did not know the cause behind my realization. At that moment my consciousness existed between reality and dreams because I was imagining occurrences which were not present.

My friend once experienced a similar sense to the one I am describing. He unexpectedly stated to his wife in the restaurant "I wonder how Dr. R. is doing in Pittsburgh" without prior mention of the doctor. Her shock occurred because she already had the same thought as he did in that instant. Weird, right? Time seemed exactly the right moment for them to ponder about Dr. R. because they had completely stopped discussing him.

The two completely missed the man before yet they both separately thought about his image at the very moment. Their minds shared exactly the same idea simultaneously as if they were in a shared reality. Even though the occurrence could not be considered supernatural the situation remained strange beyond standard comprehension.

Have you ever had a sense that something must have happened to you before though you cannot remember when? That's what we call déjà vu. A feeling strikes you when you enter a room which makes you think that you have already been there yet your memory fails you.

The illusion makes your mind believe you already existed through the particular instant or understand what will finish sooner or later. The experience creates a puzzling sensation because no amount of effort succeeds at locating its origin.

I held a conversation with someone who had the exact experience which I had. Her mind showed her every detail of the place before she entered including the house layout as well as the succeeding rooms and exterior view. The experience seemed strange to her since she had never been to that specific location before it was verified by her parents.

The experience seemed to have an emotional dimension other than its apparent connection. Thexiety she experienced with her own family during that time probably triggered emotional processing in her mind through déjà vu even though she was unaware of it.

Nonetheless these strange conscious or subconscious experiences may not evidence "supernatural" or "out there" conditions. The human brain functions through patterns observed in everyday life to describe illogical situations that occur in life.

Self-awareness is limited because our past emotions and fantasies silently influence each of these moments. Your mind gradually pulls elements together which previously remained unawares.

# XVIII
# Challenging to clarify experiences

Most people find it challenging to clarify such experiences. These mysterious fragments of our mind grab my fascination because I find them intriguing. Small pieces of forgotten knowledge remind us about hidden layers of thoughts and hidden layers of the world beyond what we notice initially. The underlying aspect in people might not be magic rather a profound part of human nature which remains mysterious to most. Life's interesting because there always remains additional discovery even within things that appear straightforward.

People sometimes encounter situations which feel familiar although they cannot identify the previous occurrence. That's what we call déjà vu. Walking into a space gives you a peculiar sensation that you have experienced it before even though you cannot remember the date. Your brain somehow forces the belief that you should recognize both future moments and previous experiences that never happened. The experience creates a strange sensation since no matter how much you attempt to recall it nothing comes to mind.

During a conversation I had once met a person who told me about our shared experience. While visiting a friend's home she entered with a deep feeling like she had been there previously. Her existence inside the house seemed to match exactly how the home appeared in detail together with the upcoming room and outside view. The experience felt strange to her since she had never been to that place before which her parents verified.

Somehow it was linked to emotional elements at its core. During that period of her life she was dealing with family troubles which her mind potentially expressed through déjà vu experiences regardless of her unconscious awareness.

Many unusual thoughts and feelings do not need to be classified as supernatural or distant because of their origin. Our minds complete our conscious understanding through snippets of remembered experiences when we lack sufficient information. Most people are unaware of the ways past emotions together with fantasies contribute to such moments. Your unconscious mind assembles hidden information which you had no awareness existed.

These matters often prove difficult to describe clearly. Their intriguing nature stems from the fact that these experiences fascinate me. Small indications exist in our lives to show the deeper aspects of thought and reality beyond our everyday awareness. We may not be dealing with actual wizardry but an unknown force operates within ourselves which remains challenging to comprehend. Life remains fascinating because there exists endless discovery inside what appears as basic elements.

Having a conversation with your friend when you want to express a thought has several problems with your communication. Your intention to deliver messages clearly occasionally meets difficulties when your words end up different from their intended meaning. A single thought sets off from your mind yet another meaning escapes your lips in a different direction. Due to the confusion between your thoughts and verbalization your messages become disintegrated. The reason behind these confusion moments remains difficult to figure out most of the time.

Such mix-ups between words as well as memory disappearance are more than ordinary errors. The words that escape from your mouth along with forgotten things originate from deep subconscious processes which you might not be conscious of. The human mind has an invisible force that controls verbal expressions even when these phrases differ from initial plans.

We think about one thing but unexpectedly blurt out something different. The talking part of your brain presents an unrelated thought that should not be connected to your intended statement. These thoughts seem to lay dormant behind the current train of thought until they effortlessly find a way to emerge. Deeper buried emotions tend to rise to the surface through such small mistakes because they are difficult to face and deal with.

People often learn significant information about hidden surface happenings through uncontrollable verbal mishaps. Memory lapses such as forgetting names or essential words in conversations show more than typical forgetfulness.

The human brain functions like a shield which prevents key information from surfacing most likely because those memories connect to avoided issues. Something uncomfortable. You should refrain from intensively pondering it. None of this is intended; your mind aims to shield you from upsetting emotions linked to past events.

People often make unintentional blunders with their speech and movements because their internal conflict creates an unpredictable tension. Your inner self insists on opposing requests from one portion of yourself to another. Within your body two contradictory drives work to take over. A silent inner voice guides you away from remembering (the memory is "not yet") despite your conscious decision to recall it (you need to remember). Not now." Your soul strives to balance out all that you wish to share with all the thoughts you constrain within.

The difficulty in remembering a resolution or changing behavior stems from conflicting impulses from within yourself. The ways of your conscious self match what your mind wants to accomplish while an unconscious element working against you leads to your failure. Your inner forces guide your decisions in ways you may never fully understand. This occurrence remains unclear although it seems these invisible powers are always present in your life.

All these brief mental interruptions represented by wrong speech and lost memories and accidental movements function as warning signs. These small slips occur when your subconscious mind attempts paranormal communication to convey vital information about yourself that you are not yet prepared to grasp. Your subconscious shows hidden truths by delivering them subconscious messages through so-called mistakes. All these accidental actions deserve more observation rather than instant dismissal. Your errors potentially reveal inner aspects about you that you have never become conscious of.

The states the truth with this comparison. Each dream adopts its very own language, which might be complicated to decode during initial interpretation. Dreams appear in exactly the same way as brief confusing mental mistakes occur during wakefulness because they contain unseen mental fragments that become disconnected in a scrambled manner.

The hidden message inside this disorder becomes visible once we excavate underneath the surface level. The unconscious part of ourselves appears to share our mental contents through different methods beyond our ability to remember. The exploration of this phenomenon becomes something essential for your attention.

Alright, let's break this down a bit. We've all experienced those moments when something just doesn't go as planned, right? Like when we accidentally say the wrong word, or do something completely out of the ordinary, and we can't really explain why. It's almost like something inside us took control for a second, right? Now, here's where it gets interesting. Those little "oops" moments—whether they're mistakes in speech, actions, or decisions—are actually a reflection of something deeper going on in our minds. And it's not just limited to sleep or dreams. These little disturbances happen when we're awake, too, and they carry meaning.

Now, think about this: when we do something wrong or make a mistake, we often just dismiss it, assuming it's some sort of malfunction or a "bad day" kind of thing. But, what if I told you that these moments aren't just random? They're actually revealing parts of our subconscious that we've tucked away and tried to forget. It's as though we've tried to lock away certain feelings or thoughts, and when we act or speak out of character, it's like those hidden emotions are sneaking through the cracks, trying to make themselves known.

The truth is, there's a thin line between what we call "normal" and "neurotic" behaviors. In fact, most of us are somewhere in between. It's like we all have a little bit of that nervous energy, those quirky actions or thoughts that feel a bit off. We're not all perfectly composed, and that's okay. We're all human. And what's fascinating is that these little missteps or unconscious actions are actually revealing how our minds are processing unresolved or repressed feelings—things that might be uncomfortable or even painful.

Think about it: the more we try to push away certain thoughts or memories, the more they start to show up in unexpected ways. It could be a slip of the tongue or a minor action that doesn't seem to make sense at the time. And yet, this is how the mind operates—pushing those feelings away from our conscious thoughts, but never completely erasing them. It's like trying to suppress a song that keeps playing in the background, even when you're not listening.

And here's the kicker—whether we're dealing with these things in small, manageable doses or in bigger, more overwhelming ways, it's all part of the same process. These unconscious forces don't just disappear because we ignore them.

They find a way to express themselves, even in subtle, seemingly insignificant ways. The beauty of it is that, by recognizing these moments, by seeing them for what they really are, we can start to better understand the deeper layers of our psyche—the parts that we often avoid or don't want to face.

So, the next time something small throws you off, don't just brush it aside. Ask yourself: what's really going on underneath the surface? What might this little slip-up be trying to tell me? It's all connected, and it's all pointing to something greater, something deeper within us that's longing for expression. And maybe, just maybe, by paying attention to these little "mistakes," we can unlock the parts of ourselves we've been trying to hide for too long.

# XIX

# The Power of Silence

Individuals wonder how silence delivers beneficial effects on their well-being. Silence beyond its calming state provides documented neurological and health advantages to the human body. Your brain faces cognitive overload and stress while developing insomnia when it constantly must process endless information because of constant noise. When experiencing true silence the brain receives time to restore itself. Reduced stress allows improved focus and enhanced brain efficiency in these conditions.

The human brain develops through the presence of silence throughout its development. Brain cell growth within the hippocampus memory region increases with only two hours of daily silence. Daily practice of silence brings benefits to learning productivity, combined with improved retention of information.

Through silence, people gain self-awareness, and it enables creative thinking to flourish. Deep quietness enables you to understand yourself better, which facilitates individual development. Your mind can experience new ideas and creative breakthroughs by allowing free thought when you decrease external disturbances.

Making room for silence in our daily life remains difficult because our world continues to provide many distractions. Listening to a quiet environment brings multiple benefits because silences create space for relaxation and enables clearer thinking while making you understand yourself better and generating new ideas.

# XX

# Finding Tranquility in a Noisy World

Understanding the advantages of silence represents only one part of acquiring the skills needed for developing it in our noisy environment. The right approach enables people to find brief instances of tranquility even though escaping day-to-day noise seems impossible at first.

Set aside minimum daily sessions devoted to quietness. A period of just five minutes will lead to apparent changes. People should spend moments of quietness during the early parts of the day before everything begins or late hours after most people settle into sleep.

A specific quiet area at home also serves as a useful setup to achieve peace. You can establish an unobstructed space for serenity which gives you time to reflect in peace. Your inner peace profoundly depends on the environments which you choose to be around.

The practice of mindfulness provides an efficient strategy which yields considerable results. You can achieve internal stillness during any circumstances by staying present to your bodily signs while eliminating disturbances from your mind.

Develop a daily habit that includes moments of silence. Spend one quiet meal each week and walk quietly and drive your car without musical or podcast entertainment. Small behavioral modifications will introduce peacefulness with increased life clarity.

Seeking periods of silence intentionally helps you achieve peace while remaining in high-pressure settings.

# XXI

## The practice of silence enables you to develop inner peace during

Seeking inner peace becomes possible through the power of silence. The underestimated power of silence serves as a means to develop tranquility so it affects your mental state as well as your physical space. Silence functions as an essential escape mechanism during hectic modern times because people must escape from noisy information overload experienced through their senses. The silencing of your inner thoughts enables concentration on real time experience while decreasing both anxiety and stress which block inner peace.

Silence also fosters mindfulness. Your acceptance of quietness allows you to develop heightened self-consciousness regarding mental and emotional states without forming theoretical opinions about them. As you discover more about yourself through self-awareness the process becomes an important path for experiencing deep peace and contentment. Open silence enables you to establish better contact with your authentic self. When you quiet external noises you become able to hear your inner voice clearly and gain an understanding about what you need and want and value in life. For a permanent state of inner peace you need to establish alignment with your genuine self.

Learning from silence enables individual self-understanding through deep introspection because it serves as a tool for internal self-reflection.

Silence acts as a powerful instrument which helps people achieve self-reflection beyond its role in creating calmness. Quiet time provides the opportunity to view deeper components of your heart and brain which otherwise blend into daily background noise. The human mind unfailingly moves toward reflections of past moments and thoughts when it experiences silent periods. The self-reflective practice enables you to gain deeper knowledge about yourself.

# XXII

# Silence as a Tool for Self-Reflection

The absence of speech creates the necessary condition you need to examine your interior with clarity. During this peaceful state, you gain the ability to look at your core beliefs alongside your life values and choice selection. Personal transformation requires accepting temporary uncomfortable states, which are essential for self-evolution. Through silence, you gain independence to analyze how you see things while you assess your current beliefs and test your inner fears and invalidate your wrongly held beliefs. During these times you attain better understanding of your decisions along with your fundamental purposes and personal direction.

Silence teaches someone to maintain patience, which allows a person to stay present with their thoughts and emotions instead of acting hastily. Emotional intelligence grows through practicing silence because it teaches you to handle emotions better while developing deeper self-knowledge and fellow human understanding.

When used as a medium, silence demonstrates the inner mental processes of your being. Using it as a guide enables people to uncover themselves better, while it enhances their personal evolution. You should open yourself to silent periods since they will help you grow into a more self-aware individual.

# XXIII

# The Healing Power of Silence

Embracing silence leads you to understand that this practice represents a deep healing power. Silence establishes itself as a retreat which safeguards people from the perpetual noise that occupies our external environment. These peaceful moments provide you with a space to renew your bond with your inner being and understand your feelings better and gain a clear perspective. This self-awareness fosters emotional healing, helping to ease stress, anxiety, and inner turmoil.

Your ability to perceive physical signals from your body becomes stronger through the power of silence. As distractions lose their hold you develop a keener ability to identify bodily tension as well as discomfort and stress symptoms that will help you tackle these issues effectively. The combination of mental and physical growth makes silence transform into a profound tool that restores balance in life.

### Strengthening Relationships Through Silence

While silence serves as an individual tool it proves equally effective for building better relationships. During emotional confrontations the practice of silence provides time to recuperate along with time to formulate deliberate responses instead of spontaneous reactions. A basic communication technique helps avoid confusion between people apart from developing respect while creating more effective communication methods.

True listening happens in silence. Utilizing silence means more than waiting to speak up since it involves actively listening to what others say while grasping their emotions and developing a better understanding of their viewpoint.

Intimacy emerges from moments during which both parties maintain quiet until they finish speaking. Silence that two people experience together serves as an indicator of mutual trust and understanding and establishes a deep emotional bond. The necessary element is maintaining balance because silence must not serve to establish distance in relationships. The right implementation of silence with active appreciation creates an influential method to enhance relationships while forging deeper connections between people.

## The Art of Active Listening

The ability to actively listen represents a strong skill that drives significant improvement in all your relationships. Listening actively means more than silent attention during a conversation since it demands that you devote complete commitment and interpretation of another person's viewpoint before responding with sincere involvement in the dialogue.

Active listening means more than just hearing words since it requires high-end interpretation of meaning combined with visible body language detection and purposeful replies. The process functions as two ways because you both receive and offer inputs to the communication through various forms of contact and meaningful responses. You prove respect and caregiving behavior when you choose to understand alternative viewpoints regardless of agreement.

Learning active listening techniques allows you to enhance interpersonal connections by fixing communication problems and fixing conflicts together with strengthening relationships. Practicing with patience and genuine interest creates priceless rewards through the development of trustworthy and understanding connections between people.

## Silence and Emotional Well-being

Active listening helps strengthen human relationships but emotional well-being requires the necessary presence of silence. Your emotional core requires the missing silence to process its feelings which grants you the needed mental clarity.

A period without sound functions as an automatic method to reduce stress levels. Prolonged exposure to conversation from both outside sources and within your mind leads to increased anxiety levels. Creating tranquil moments lets you build sacred spaces in which stress disappears hence establishing emotional stability. Mindfulness becomes possible through silence because it allows you to remain present while avoiding thoughts about past experiences and future concerns. This mindful presence fosters a sense of peace and contentment.

Silence should not confuse people into thinking it means avoiding others in life. The purpose of silence in life is to permit yourself proper engagement with your thoughts in sustainable ways that support healing. Through purposeful practice of silence you develop stronger emotional resilience simultaneously strengthening your personal connection to your inner self.

**Spiritual maturity emerges through the practice of silence as demonstrated.**

Silence provides both external features and offers a spiritual pathway which leads to personal transformation. The noisy world gives us silence as a sacred sanctuary to explore our spiritual depths through which we discover ourselves.

People seek silence as an act of deliberate concentration which both calms thoughts and emotion but also makes room for self-knowledge. Silent contemplation enables you to study your beliefs and values as well as your life purpose thus strengthening your knowledge of self and spiritual development. Various spiritual traditions consider silence as an essential element to develop mindfulness and presence which leads people toward connection with transcendent powers.

Practicing silence helps you achieve both internal relaxation and emotional stability as well as synchronization with the environmental patterns. Within this peaceful time true wisdom emerges together with transformative growth which leads toward spiritual growth and enhances your sense of completeness.

## The Calming Effect of Silence on Stress

The reduction of stress steps in synchrony with silence to create a state of relaxation. The continuous exposure to noise which characterizes the current fast-paced world creates higher stress levels in people. When people welcome peace through silence it functions as a natural method for stress management which in turn leads to healthier blood pressure levels and better sleep quality as well as stronger immune response. Investigative evidence demonstrates how brain relaxation happens during quie time enabling it to bypass superfluous sensory information processing.

Silence enhances both emotional management abilities and assists people in learning better ways to handle future difficulties. Inner peace requires noise minimization together with deliberate slowing down of life activities. People who make regular room for silence in their routines find both mental rest and personal revelation which improves their total health state.

# XXIV

# Maximizing Productivity Through Silence

Using silence as a tool creates enhanced efficiency and concentration levels in people. The advantage of removing diversions allows people to create optimum settings for profound concentration. The human brain requires deep work states to find solutions while being creative and we achieve this intensive focus through maintaining quiet environments that cut out endless notifications and electronic disturbances. Several steps should be established to benefit from quiet time effectively. People can begin their day in complete silence, after which they should implement noise-blocking technology and choose an uninterrupted workspace. The practice of developing such habits creates pathways to better productivity levels and improved mental awareness.

## *The Role of Silence in Enhancing Sleep Quality*

Restful rest depends on silence so people maintain their mental and physical wellness. During sleep the brain continues its operations by processing incoming sounds which generate disruptions in rest. Establishing a silent sleeping environment prevents interruptions so people experience better and more healing slumber. Scientific studies demonstrate that being in a silence-free environment reduces stress, making people both sleep more quickly and sleep better. The absence of noise before sleep aids in regulating the sleep hormone melatonin. Nighttime silence provides individuals with major benefits to their sleep quality together with their total well-being.

## *You will find the entryway to intuition within silence during*

One can better receive intuitive messages through silence because it strengthens their connection to subconscious awareness. A state of silence reduces external disturbances that make way for instinctive thoughts along with emotions to emerge. The public sees intuition as a built-in navigation system which gets erased through everyday noises. Establishing a period of quietness enables people to enhance their mental concentration while developing their ability to make better choices. When practiced self-reflection becomes possible, which leads people to understand emotional and experiential levels of themselves better. The act of silence transforms into an effective way to achieve both understanding and clarity.

## *Silence and Physical Well-being*

Silence provides benefits for physical health apart from its effects on mental well-being. Prolonged noise exposure causes stress elevation together with increased blood pressure while creating higher cortisol levels in the body. Daily silence periods in our life activate relaxation responses in our body which decrease stress-induced health problems. Studies show that silent environments stimulate new hippocampal cell growth because the hippocampus drives memory and learning functions. Silence helps strengthen immune functions thus enabling the body to mend and protect itself against illnesses. Individuals who accept silence will improve their physical health and mental well-being.

## *Finding Strength in Solitude*

Many people mistake solitude for loneliness even though this solitary state proves beneficial for personal development. Serving silence as an active practice enables an individual to build reflection about themselves and creative imagination. The quiet times enable a person to develop deeper perceptions about their thoughts and emotions along with their dreams. The absence of outside interruptions during periods of solitude motivates many intellectuals and creative minds to generate fresh inspirations. People should accept solitude as an occasion to find themselves and achieve inner tranquility instead of labeling it as isolated solitude.

## Silence as a Form of Self-Care

Self-Care finds representation through the practice of remaining silent with oneself.

People should create silent moments to achieve valuable mental recovery along with caring for themselves. Despite constant environmental stimulation people need quiet periods to lower stress and create improved health. Scientific research demonstrates that periods of quietness decrease heart rate together with blood pressure levels and stress hormone production which enables both mental clarity and relaxation.

Timing away from noise helps people explore their mental activities thus they gain more command of their emotional responses while making wiser choices about their decisions. Regularly practicing silence within daily activities leads people to establish a life which feels balanced and complete.

## The Art of Letting Go Through Silence

Through silence, people obtain a chance to remove mental weight while creating possibilities for self-improvement. The mental disruption that noise creates matches the weight that people feel from unresolved emotions combined with unneeded worries. Restful contemplation enables people to recognize emotions and process them, which creates emotional strength. Open embrace of silence enables people to release their stress and past regrets and unrealistic expectations, so they can welcome fresh experiences with new perspectives. Using this practice serves the purpose of developing mental space rather than it being a method to escape reality.

## The Role of Silence in Conflict Resolution

When conflicts arise silence functions as a strong instrument that leads to conflict resolution. Reactionally speaking immediately will lose its place when you silence your thoughts while gaining understanding about alternative viewpoints. Silence creates a serene environment that reduces tensions between people during unstable moments. The practice enables active hearing between people because it creates opportunities for uninterrupted attention to other voices. The inclusion of silence in discussions enables people to develop stronger relationships and find peaceful conflict resolutions and to build empathy among participants.

## *Using Silence to Enhance Communication*

Business intelligence experts commonly view silence as a lack of communication although in actual practice it functions as an essential ingredient for meaningful exchanges. Taking time to reflect before speaking helps people produce more deliberate messages that achieve better results in communication.

Chatting with silence helps people pay attention to what others say and this practice communicates respect that strengthens interpersonal bonds. Non-verbal indicators used properly can create heavier impact during communication enabling more successful conversations. Effective use of silence brings better results for both relationships with friends and colleagues.

## *Personal Growth Through Silence*

Self-discovery and personal development happen when people use silence as their trigger. The quickly moving lifestyle tends to drown people with environmental noise which causes them to forget their life goals and core beliefs. Quiet intervals provide people with time to unite with their internal nature which leads to enhanced awareness and individual development. The practice of embracing silence leads people toward better self-awareness which helps them make solid decisions and see their life's true priorities better. The practice of silence produces much more than noiseless surroundings because it enables inner peace and transformation as well as personal growth.

# XXV
## INTRODUCTION TO MINDFULNESS

People are like stained-glass windows. These objects become more beautiful as darkness arrives only when light illuminates them from inside.

**Understanding Mindfulness**

As a practice, we engage our entire awareness to the present moment through observing our movements while thinking processes appear and experiencing our emotions unfold. Through consistent practice and focus mindfulness improves our perceptiveness together with strengthening our compassion toward ourselves along with our fellow humans.

You should always carry with you the endless options which childhood used to offer.

The world during childhood appeared to hold an unlimited number of potential opportunities. Our days exceeded normal bounds so holidays persisted indefinitely and peaceful nighttime rest gave us power for upcoming adventures. The morning greeted us with enthusiasm, while evening brought satisfaction.

When did life transform into its current state? The requirements of maturity arrived when we needed employment and income to support ourselves and possibly care for a family. It could have begun in school under exam stress that forced students to stay up late while consuming caffeine and stimulating themselves with stress.

Many people face a tiresome repeating pattern that causes them to believe stress belongs to the natural structure of living.

### Work-related stress requires a mental change of perspective.

The possibility to recover this feeling exists. The day should bring opportunities which transcend performing duties. Working environment would become motivating instead of draining work procedures.

Your initial doubt arises because you perceive work as something you accept without enthusiasm. Does every job as an employee turn into continuing hardship while delivering minimal future benefits?

## PRACTICAL MINDFULNESS

### Embracing Mindfulness in Daily Life

People without personal choices experience lost meaning in their existence.

According to some people working under the supervision of another party delivers all benefits directly to the employer. When power dominances exist at work employees typically feel less important. Mandated hierarchical pressure paths upward through the organization to affect leadership roles even though they must endure it from above.

There are many workers who experience low value and detachment from their workplace duties. A different viewpoint about this matter should be possible. Our ability to address challenges relating to identity and worldview may emerge from viewing ourselves and our position differently.

### Welcome to the Modern Era

Organizational and commercial sectors show increasing rapid changes that create unprecedented stress for professionals in the workforce. The relentless pressure leads employees to experience reduced focus together with mental exhaustion while causing them to lose interest more frequently.

Medical experts have maintained their emphasis on the stress-related effects on bodily health throughout this period. Medical experts recognize the inseparable link between persistent stress and the development of multiple medical conditions including high blood pressure as well as heart disease and obesity together with diabetes and anxiety depression and cancer.

The Information Age represents our current era where people enjoy unlimited data access through digital connections which exist in perpetuity. People obtain new capabilities through technology but stand under continuous digital stimuli. Most people feel restricted by their daily use of desktops laptops and smartphones throughout the entire day.

Although human brains demonstrate intense adaptability, they do not possess the capabilities of mechanical systems. The key to managing life in the fast lane involves developing both a balanced and resilient mind because this "human software" helps achieve life satisfaction without experiencing stress.

## *Mindfulness: An Ancient Wisdom*

Mindfulness exists as an ancient practice. Approximately 2500 years ago Buddha noted how the mind has greater strength than people understand while all things derive their origin from thought.

Most people maintain an unsettled state of mind throughout their daily activities as their thoughts transition between unorganized and unfocused streams. The Monkey Mind experience appears likewise to what a monkey does by jumping between different trees without direction. An uncontrolled stream of mental thought produces stress and distraction as its end result.

Mindfulness helps people learn to accept their current circumstances without resisting them. Unforced experience acceptance leads to stress reduction which automatically produces both clarity and inner peace.

A Practice and a Mindset

Researchers have established that mindful meditation as a practice regularly improves our ability to handle stress and develops our emotions toward compassion and empathy. The emotional regulation training through mindfulness enables people to transform negative reactions into positive emotional experience.

Through mindfulness practice the fight-or-flight response becomes calmer thus our brain can access the prefrontal cortex for rational thinking and decision-making. Mindfulness functions as a habitual daily routine and a fundamental change in mental awareness.

Our ability to concentrate grows through mindful breathing practice that also creates an internal state of tranquility. The skill of heightened awareness provides us with the ability to use creativity for problem-solving and improve our communication, which benefits both personal development and career success.

## THE MIND IS LIKE SOFTWARE – PROTECT IT FROM VIRUSES!

Your mind operates like computer software thus you need protection from destructive elements.

The purpose of mindfulness directs us to purposefully focus attention on current experiences while we maintain non-judgmental awareness towards them. Research studies today confirm that mindfulness amounts to a fundamental component for reaching happiness.

The practice of mindfulness spans more than two thousand years even though it presents as a modern concept today. Science demonstrates the importance of mindfulness development in improving fundamental life attributes. The process of managing mindfulness requires both patience combined with regular practice. The absence of a successful technique requires you to stop and choose another method. The main objective requires maintaining an active mental presence and complete involvement in the present moment.

### The Science Behind Mindfulness

The Conscious and Subconscious Mind

Mindfulness becomes easier to comprehend when we study its relationship with two essential mind functions: Consciousness and Subconsciousness.

We can understand the mind through comparison with software.

The Conscious Mind operates like the daily apps which handle present activities and outside communications.

The Subconscious Mind behaves as an automatic operating system which maintains background operations to store data and manipulate unnoticeable actions.

### The Conscious Mind: The Active Interface

External stimuli enter our brain through its processing system before the conscious mind receives and interprets the information. The conscious mind functions as our aware mental unit which holds onto our movements and internal reactions as well as our surrounding environment in present time.

In our relationship with the world and ourselves the conscious mind functions by generating speech expression along with movements and writing actions as well as using imagery and thoughts. The system functions in a similar way to smartphones since basic memory retrieval occurs through application access for important recall functions such as phoning numbers or recalling names. The system enables users to handle daily behaviors together with standard thoughts in the same way it handles background applications.

## *The Subconscious Mind: The Hidden Operating System*

Deep-seated behaviors along with beliefs and emotions reside within the subconscious area of the mind which people seldom recognize. Long-term memory storage occurs in this mental domain since the beginning of birth. As computers are prone to viruses so are the human mind.

Our lives quietly transform because of negative thought patterns and mental conditioning that we describe as "viruses." Such mental problems appear without reason yet they create feelings of powerlessness and a lack of understanding regarding their source. Through mindfulness practice we can discover and eliminate such mental obstacles which help enhance our psychological health.

# XXVI

# The Hidden Storehouse of Memories

The subconscious mind functions as a grand repository for hiding distant recollections of past events which fall into two groups: unconscious remnant memories and traumatic repressed memories. Even though we are not aware of it these stored memories direct how we think and behave through our habits and beliefs.

Memory blocks emerge from the subconscious when familiar smells or specific melodies or returning to places from childhood produce these unexpected recollections. Deep psychological techniques including hypnosis produce the ability to recover hidden memories. A stimulus or retrieval method serves as the necessary requirement to bring subconscious information to our conscious mind.

The subconscious part of our mind functions autonomously because it manages automatic psychological activities that affect emotional responses and instinctive behaviors and choose how we make decisions. Our subconscious communicates the world to us primarily through feelings along with imagination and dreams and physical sensations to protect our survival.

The method ensures survival by following proven strategies from previous experiences which were beneficial before our modern era. Most human activities follow established patterns although these patterns might no longer be beneficial.

# *The Iceberg Analogy: Conscious vs. Subconscious Mind*

Standing on the surface of the water, you can see only a portion of an iceberg as it floats at sea. The conscious mind operates from the small visible piece at the top while managing rational decisions as well as awareness. The part of the iceberg underwater represents the subconscious mind which remains hidden yet controls most aspects of human life.

An iceberg's massive hidden part beneath the water directs ships, while our subconscious mechanisms embed past beliefs that control and obstruct us without our conscious knowledge. The process of recognizing hidden mental influences leads toward constructive change.

Mindfulness and Self-Awareness

According to emotional intelligence definition, "**a person requires knowledge about their mental experience alongside recognition of personal tastes along with personal capabilities and automatic mental responses.**" We need to monitor our emotions and thoughts when they occur because this proves their critical importance.

Emotional intelligence starts from building awareness about oneself. Observing our real-time thoughts and emotions enables better self-understanding, with an opportunity to achieve inner peace while we voluntarily control our actions.

Individuals who understand themselves well make decisions before acting without impulse. Such individuals maintain strong psychological health alongside positive life views while establishing deep compassionate relationships with people.

Our training in mindfulness creates stronger self-awareness capabilities that enable us to eliminate restricting beliefs and choose consciously while we achieve better life direction and intent.

**Looking Inward**

Our mindful state is linked to the aware part of our mind which remains active during moments of mindfulness practice. The conscious mind leads our attention and keeps focus, while also displaying the capability to visualize beyond actual reality.

People show different levels of positive thinking because some were born with this talent but others have inner mental patterns from their early years that make thinking positive difficult. Human beings have access to an extraordinary ability that allows them to guide their focused awareness.

Real transformation in our lives depends on our ability to steer our mental focus correctly. Controlling the focus of attention is the fundamental element of mindfulness. Our destiny unfolds through two essential choices, which include evaluating our thinking patterns and regulating the mental entry of specific thoughts. When we control our thoughts we modify subconscious mind processes which removes restriction beliefs while eliminating patterned negativity.

Regular mindfulness exercises teach us to restructure the subconscious mind which leads to better beliefs and enhanced mental independence. The process of understanding this concept makes us stronger in our ability to choose and craft significant decisions for our lives.

## Choosing to vs. Having to

Society follows two essential pillars namely culture and religion, thus both systems function as controlling structures to provide guidance for human organization. People see cultural patterns in different ways since they either help or limit personal growth. The same applies to fields like science, medicine, politics, and education.

The numerous mental and temporal commitments make it seem practical to submit our decisions to outside influences regarding food consumption and medicine usage and thinking processes as well as clothing and marital matters. The expectations of our society force us to battle for mental freedom together with physical autonomy and mental autonomy.

People choose to follow tested conduct methods without checking whether those methods make sense. A daughter witnessed her mother trimming pot roast ends when preparing dinner so she developed the habit of doing it herself. The girl deduced that she was observing a culinary practice when her mother trimmed both ends. The woman eventually understood her ongoing behavior when she recalled she had never paused to think about it since her mother conducted it for matching her small cooking pot.

A brief story demonstrates the way people easily advance through their lives by performing actions they do not comprehend fully and their actual significance.

The success of consumer culture depends on how people compulsively pursue social norms even though they understand it makes no sense. Every day new advertisements demonstrate the constant drive for people to obtain bigger more luxurious things that are shinier and different from the old ones.

Survival shows present selected segments of celebrity existence so it appears we have personal access to their lives. People spend their screen time watching trivial life updates from their contacts through social media platforms.

They only do not follow trends if they possess an independent mindset. People sometimes cross their threshold when they become aware of their false existence and announce their definitive decision to stop.

# XXVII
# Making Conscious Choices

The choice-oriented statement "I choose to" gives people the power to replace statements "I should," "I must," and "I have to." The shift from feeling obligated to having autonomy through language change enables us to solve problems with innovation.

Taking responsibility for our choices enables us to release victimhood patterns and start developing ourselves as individuals. The foundation of achieving mindfulness starts from selecting personal decisions rather than feeling compelled to meet obligations.

## For example:

The statement changes from "I accept this job because money is necessary" into "I actively seek superior opportunities across the upcoming weeks."

I am committed to discover different methods that will enhance my health because doctors alone are not responsible for my medical condition.

Better communication skills development is what I select as my primary choice.

## Mindful Commitments

Strengthening our mindfulness involves changing our passive selection methods to active decision-making processes.

Examples of 'I Choose To...'

Eat healthier meals.

Prioritize my well-being.

Accept and embrace my body.

I request everyone to value my experience from growing older.

I focus more awareness on my mental processing.

Further my education.

Pursue a fulfilling career.

Encourage my children's independence.

My intention is to pardon my parents despite their failures.

Show kindness to my colleagues.

Look for positive aspects in both people together with environmental circumstances.

I will take ownership of my entire life.

**Examples of 'I Resolve To...'**

Adopt a healthier diet.

Quit smoking and harmful habits.

Maintain a balanced weight.

Engage in regular exercise.

Meditate consistently.

Enroll in further education.

Seek better employment opportunities.

I need to show greater patience when I interact with my relatives.

Avoid gossip and negativity.

Accept what I cannot change.

I should examine new medical and therapeutic methods for wellness.

Understanding Stress, Depression, and Mindfulness

The Impact of Stress on Mental Health and Relationships

Depression risks significantly increase due to chronic stress but only when people fail to find effective stress management.

Stress management issues in people create mood problems which reduce work performance and strain relationships and cause sleep difficulties.

People usually overlook stress at first until it transforms their personal relationships.

Clinical social worker Judy Ford explains that stress acts like an infection passing between partners with the same pattern as ping-pong until it causes relationship disputes followed by withdrawal and relationship separation.

The combination of prolonged stress leads to both conditions of depression as well as emotional detachment from others.

Everybody holds traces of personal dissatisfaction which represents carrying weight from past events.

People tend to miss present-time fulfillment when regret strikes because they lack satisfaction in their desires.

People desire enough strength to demonstrate their true selves.

Regretting excessive work commitments.

Failing to express emotions.

Losing touch with friends.

People deprive themselves of happiness even when it is accessible to them.

Immune system decline due to stress finally leads to serious health problems including heart disease and stroke as well as cancer.

When stress takes hold us we tend to make hasty irrational decisions which may affect our choices badly.

The Power of Mindfulness

Mindfulness functions as a treatment for stress because it promotes peaceful presence.

Such practice demands selecting objectives every day which synchronize unconscious thoughts with conscious behaviors.

Mindfulness practice requires one to be present while turning into a state of attentive awareness which keeps our actions intentional rather than automatic.

A person who practices mindfulness understands they will never reach perfection thus they dedicate themselves to lifelong improvement through curiosity and compassion.

## Applying Mindfulness in Daily Life

Start the Day with Intention

Set the daily schedule during evening time for the following day.

Focusing the workspace through proper organization allows for better clarity and attention.

Social media engagement needs regulation by time boundaries.

## Practice Gratitude Upon Waking

Before sleeping find time to thank everyday basics such as comfortable living conditions and loved ones and available opportunities.

Treat optimistic events along with difficult situations as chances for growth.

People who show gratitude experience mental clarity that creates a positive atmosphere at the beginning of each day.

Observation of people and environments should be combined with understanding of others' emotional states.

People should demonstrate emotional understanding during their professional duties and while interacting with people they know personally.

Spend no time thinking about grievances and negative thoughts specifically when performing daily activities such as taking a shower or traveling.

Mindfulness practice enables people to eliminate negative behaviors triggered by stress while building better relationships which leads to a contented life without stress. Making careful small modifications brings about major life transformations regarding both health and happiness.

To practice mindfulness means being fully focused on the present moment while developing awareness through an experience that requires no evaluation or criticism. Through mindfulness practice in everyday life people establish better relationships between their awareness of mental processes and emotional awareness and their environment.

## The Essence of Mindfulness

Mindfulness helps people watch their thoughts and feelings while keeping away from becoming overcome by them. Instead of living in the past or future individuals redirect their focus to the present. The practice helps individuals obtain clearer mind and emotional balance.

## Techniques to Cultivate Mindfulness

Observing your breath in its natural state enables you to focus your mind which results in calmness.

Through Body Scan Meditation people learn to focus their attention on their body parts which results in tension release while enhancing their body awareness.

A practice that involves grateful reflection about positive aspects of life leads to stronger emotional well-being and better appreciation.

The practice of mindful eating involves total attention to food senses for forming better eating habits.

Walking Meditation provides grounding through slow deliberate movements which focus on the individual steps to connect your mind to present circumstances.

## Benefits of Mindfulness

Regular practice of mindfulness leads to important health advances that impact mental functioning as well as emotional state and physical well-being. Some key benefits include:

## Reduced stress and anxiety

Enhanced focus and concentration
Improved emotional regulation
Greater self-awareness
Increased resilience to challenges
Integrating Mindfulness into Daily Life
People who want to practice mindfulness in daily life should begin with these strategies:

Deep breathing and meditation practice for a few minutes should be your first action of the day.

Brief breaks in your daily schedule should involve checking both your mental and emotional condition.

People struggling with stress should partake in activities that include writing in journals or listening to relaxing melodies or spending time outdoors.

People should eliminate interruptions while working on single assignments.

Show kindness to others and compassion to yourself through the rejection of self-criticism.

## A Holistic Approach to Challenges

Applying an expanded frame of reference brings advantages in difficult circumstances. Recent studies confirm that focus and mental orientation create significant effects upon our life experiences.

Drawing away from direct engagement allows us to achieve better understanding regarding our challenges. It helps to ask ourselves:

To what extent did I create this scenario?

I was partially unaware of every detail in the process.

Do I have opportunities to alter my perspective which could benefit the result?

Under which circumstances did I allow the issue to progress?

The practice of mindfulness reveals answers related to several core elements.

Fear of embracing change.

A rigid mindset.

People tend to make decisions through reactions linked to their past while neglecting current situation evaluation.

Shifting blame onto others.

A distracted and unfocused mind.

The experiences we have accumulated so far define our present identity but they will not determine the way we will develop in the future. Getting knowledge from challenging experiences is essential but emotional attachment should stay out of it.

Acceptance of guidance alongside humility remains a demanding challenge for most people. Individuals commonly avoid this process because they wish to avoid looking weak and showing their mistakes or preserving their image. The start of responsibility ownership comes from self-identification in situations which lead us toward taking charge.

## *The Victim Mentality*

Some of my friends possess all the qualities of intelligence along with kindness and humor. The social media messages they post exhibit a combination of engaging wit and understanding which makes their audience deeply love them.

Various social media posts from these platforms focus on complaints as their main content. People use social media to express frustration about terrible colleagues and unkind customers along with aggravating supervisors and small matters such as unfavorable precipitation. Through their message they express a helpless feeling because life continues to bring challenges to them.

The content of their social media posts has led me to consider asking them directly about taking control over their disliked life aspects. Why should you assume responsibility only for items that create happiness yet refuse it for challenges?

Combatting victimhood lies within the practice of mindfulness. Mindfulness grants us the freedom to overcome stress as well as frustration and dependency through thoughts that seek solutions instead of dwelling on complaints.

## *Rising Above Adversity*

People facing severe difficulties exist in problem areas where they suffer through poverty or illness or encounter oppression. The resilience of certain people becomes extraordinary when they maintain their composure through unbearable situations.

People find it challenging to maintain composure when they experience exhaustion together with fear and loss of hope. Some individuals display this ability yet many people lose their composure under similar circumstances. Why?

Some experts believe that both personality characteristics and mental vision capabilities are important factors in reaching success. Before they began their pursuit many people who fled from daunting circumstances originally pictured alternative futures in their mind. Human beings succeed through years of captivity to return as people who demonstrate both strength and determination and purpose within life.

**The key factor? The power of the mind.**

## *The Journey to Mindfulness*

The concept of mindfulness appears advanced to individuals who have little exposure to it. The principles of this philosophy will lead you to discover specific methods that help decrease stress together with the ability to become happier. When individuals start taking any measure of positive action they produce substantial meaningful changes.

The practice of mindfulness disrupts the fundamental beliefs people possess about religion along with their learning system and public customs.

Mindfulness presents itself as a demand for people to escape their comfort range while taking control of their lived moments. We should not shame ourselves for everything that occurs yet we need to become aware of how our subconscious thoughts and behaviors shape our life experiences.

Several people struggle to accept this approach. People wonder what reason exists for personally introducing anxiety or stress to their lives. The subconscious mind functions as the source behind how reality shapes our existence although we remain unaware of this influence. The human mind processes mental patterns even though people might not detect those patterns.

Our subconscious operates like a background system of a computer as it influences everything we encounter without our conscious awareness.

## The Good News

The positive aspect which comes with this moment of realization is our ability to make changes. Being aware of our thoughts enables us to take control which leads to controlling our life. Through rewriting our life story we gain the power to make our own choices for personal creation of our dreamed reality.

The achievement of this requires mindfulness to maintain focused presence while staying calm. The process needs careful patience along with self-forgiveness alongside a commitment to unlearn societal brainwashing from the past years.

With rising awareness new prospects start to unveil themselves. Barriers which first seem like obstacles end up developing into creative challenges that help individuals develop.

## Consider these real-life examples:

A problem presents the potential for opportunity in every situation.

Mindfulness requires us to switch from rash reactions to calm observation and productive learning before distancing ourselves from confusion instead of falling into it.

Evidence can be found through practical test of the exercises so perform them to experience transformation yourself. Durability combined with dedication towards your development will guide you as your life evolves.

*Namaste.*

# Final Thoughts

The content within this work should have sparked your interest if you read it until the end. A single sentence or question together with the strong intuition that life contains more depth than we were instructed about. The impact of whatever appeared to fascinate you should continue resting within your thoughts. I hope this text presents the best challenge for your life. People do not discover an absolute truth through reality because it consists of dynamic experiential elements that result from the interplay between perception thought and awareness. Close this book while requesting from you a single request only: Do not look for answers. Look for presence. Pay attention to the voids which separate your thoughts. Notice the peaceful mental state that has been present all along despite mental distractions. The actual beginning of reality might exist in those places.